MEN

OF

VALOR

MEN

OF

VALOR

*The Powerful Impact
of a Righteous Man*

ROBERT L. MILLET

DESERET
BOOK

SALT LAKE CITY, UTAH

Library of Congress Cataloging-in-Publication Data

Millet, Robert L.
  Men of valor : the powerful impact of a righteous man / Robert L. Millet.
    p. cm.
  Includes bibliographical references and index.
  ISBN-10 1-59038-711-2 (hardbound : alk. paper)
  ISBN-13 978-1-59038-711-5 (hardbound : alk. paper)
  1. Priesthood—Church of Jesus Christ of Latter-day Saints. 2. Church of Jesus Christ of Latter-day Saints—Doctrines. I. Title.
  BX8659.M55 2007
  248.8'42088289332—dc22   2006032799

Printed in the United States of America
R. R. Donnelley and Sons, Crawfordsville, IN

10 9 8 7 6 5 4

Rise up, O men of God!
Have done with lesser things.
Give heart and soul and mind and strength
To serve the King of Kings.

Rise up, O men of God,
In one united throng.
Bring in the day of brotherhood
And end the night of wrong.

Rise up, O men of God!
Tread where his feet have trod.
As brothers of the Son of Man,
Rise up, O men of God!

(*Hymns*, no. 324)

CONTENTS

INTRODUCTION

At a time in the history of ancient Israel, perhaps a time not too different from our own, the children of Israel found themselves in bondage to the Midianites, a neighboring nation whose influence was anything but good. Because God Almighty loves his covenant people and because he keeps his promises to Abraham, Isaac, and Jacob, once again he sought to deliver the Israelites out of the prevailing darkness of the day into his marvelous light. Jehovah then did what he so often does to awaken and retrieve his wandering sons and daughters: he called upon a man—a common man, a good man—and then empowered and qualified and prepared that good man for greatness. An angel appeared to one Gideon "and said unto him, *The Lord is with thee, thou mighty man of valour*" (Judges 6:7–12; emphasis added). Gideon was then taught and shaped and readied to save his people and return them to the worship of Jehovah. With three hundred fighting men, Gideon and his small band leaned and relied wholly upon the Lord of Sabaoth, the Lord of Hosts, the

Lord of Armies, and defeated one hundred and twenty thousand of their enemies (see Judges 8:10). Yes, Gideon was a "mighty man of valor." *Valor* represents bravery and strength of character, boldness, and fortitude—all qualities that prepare a person to act responsibly in times of need, of challenge, or of danger.

A colleague of mine spent several days in a large metropolitan city, one that has a reputation for its blatant wickedness and especially its immorality. He returned home from his research trip exhausted, worn down, both emotionally and spiritually. He described painfully what he saw and especially what he felt, how the power of sin was so thick in the air one could almost slice it with a knife. "I couldn't finish up and get home fast enough," he said, in essence. "I wanted to hug my wife and children, go to Church, take the sacrament, hear the gospel preached. Most important," he added with an almost frightened look in his eye, "I wanted to pray. I wanted to plead for strength to resist, to importune the Lord for courage on the part of my children and grandchildren to stand boldly against the rising tide of evil in our time."

Truly, as the revelations attest, "the enemy is combined" (D&C 38:12), and modern Israel's righteous force will be successful in deflecting the fiery darts of the adversary only to the extent that the men of God take their rightful place as "mighty men of valor."

The priesthood is the power and authority of God, delegated to men on earth, to act in all things pertaining to the salvation of the human family. It is God's power, loaned for a season to you and me, to make a difference in a world that desperately needs it. It is the Almighty's authorization, a divine investiture of authority, to bless people and preserve goodness and decency in our society. And it is the same power held by Him after whom the priesthood is named (D&C 107:3). As Elder Bruce R. McConkie reminded us: "We can stand in the place and stead of the Lord Jesus Christ in administering salvation to the children of men. He preached the gospel; so can we. He spoke by the power of the Holy Ghost; so can we. He served as a missionary; so can we. He went about doing good; so can we. He performed the ordinances of salvation; so can we. He kept the commandments; so can we. He wrought miracles; such also is our privilege if we are true and faithful in all things. We are his agents; we represent him; we are expected to do and say what he would do and say if he personally were ministering among men at this time" (Conference Report, October 1977, 50).

If ever there was a time, if ever there was a season, if ever there was a cause that cried out for men of purpose and men of purity to step forward and draw upon the powers of heaven, it is today. It's true that priesthood is neither male nor female, neither man nor woman. Priesthood is an authority, a divine power, a force for good in the earth and in heaven. With but two exceptions—being ordained to offices within the priesthood and performing priesthood ordinances—the women of the Church are entitled to every blessing of the priesthood that men are. Our Holy Father is no respecter of persons, and he certainly loves his daughters as much as he loves his sons. But the God of us all expects those who have been ordained to stand in the office to which they have been called; to take up their cross daily—to deny themselves of ungodliness and every worldly lust (see JST Matthew 16:24; compare Moroni 10:32); to occupy their minds with uplifting thoughts, to ponder upon that which is true, honest, just, pure, lovely, of good report, virtuous, and worthy of praise (see Philippians 4:8); to avoid places and influences and even people that would degrade or dilute the power of the priesthood; to rise up and reach out to make a difference; and to allow the holy priesthood to be felt and enjoyed by every member of the family, thereby creating within the home a bit of heaven on earth.

President Boyd K. Packer, in addressing the J. Reuben Clark Law Society at Brigham Young University, charged the assembled group: "You who hold the priesthood must be exemplars above reproach. And I charge each of you . . . and put you on alert: These are days of great spiritual danger for this people. The world is spiraling downward at an ever-quickening pace. *I am sorry to tell you that it will not get better. I know of nothing in the history of the Church or in the history of the world to compare with our present circumstances. Nothing happened in Sodom and Gomorrah which exceeds the wickedness and depravity which surrounds us now*" ("On the Shoulders of Giants," 7; emphasis added).

President Gordon B. Hinckley likewise stated: "No one need tell you that we are living in a very difficult season in the history of the world. Standards are dropping everywhere. Nothing seems to be sacred any more. . . . The traditional family is under heavy attack. *I do not know that things were worse in the times of Sodom and Gomorrah.* At that season, Abraham bargained with the Lord to save these cities for the sake of the righteous. Notwithstanding his pleas, things were so bad that Jehovah decreed their destruction. They and their wicked inhabitants were annihilated. We see similar conditions today. They prevail across the world. Our Father must weep as He looks down upon His wayward sons and daughters. In the Church we are working very hard to stem the tide of evil. But it is an uphill battle" (Worldwide Leadership Training Broadcast, 10 January 2004, 20; emphasis added).

This short book is about the priesthood and about the men who are called to hold it. It is intended to awaken us, to nudge our consciences, to educate our desires, to call us to higher ground, and to provoke us to glimpse and grasp the power with which we have been endowed. It is intended to raise a warning voice and also to sound the battle cry. We must not be naïve: we are at war, and Satan and his minions will do all they can to weaken, distract, confuse, or pollute the agents of the Lord. This must not happen. There is too much at stake, too many souls to save, too much truth to spread, too much evil to conquer. The "mighty men of valor" prepared and raised up to engage the enemy of our souls must stand and deliver. Jesus Christ is the Lord of Sabaoth, the Lord of Hosts, and the Captain of our salvation. He will not desert us in a time of growing darkness. If we will let him, he will shine his kindly and Kingly light upon us and through us. The time to step forward and be counted is now. Borrowing the words of a letter written by Joseph Smith to the Saints in Nauvoo, "Brethren, shall we not go on in so great a cause? Go forward and not backward. Courage, brethren; and on, on to the victory!" (D&C 128:22).

RISE UP!

I CAN DISTINCTLY REMEMBER sitting on the edge of my mother's bed when I was ten years old. I was overcome with a feeling of gloom, and my mother sensed it. "What's wrong?" she asked. "Oh, I don't know for sure," I said. "I'm just feeling really, really sad." As moms do so well, she managed to pry out of me what was at the heart of my heart. I finally responded: "Mama, I don't want to grow up. I want to stay ten years old forever." She looked at me with puzzled eyes and inquired: "Why, son? Why don't you want to grow up?"

I had thought about this matter a great deal and was able to reply rather quickly: "It just seems so tough to be a man. Daddy works so hard and is gone so much with his job. Uncle Joseph works at the Standard Oil long, long hours, and he just seems to hate every day of it." (I would later come to appreciate the fact that my uncle's complaints were actually expressions of how much he loved working there.) "Grandpa Millet works there too, and he has to ride his bicycle to work, and between working all night and spending much of the day building our new chapel, he looks run down. And he gets sick a lot. And then there are those men who don't have jobs. You know, the ones that come by our house all the time and ask for something to eat. They look so lonely. Mama, I like being ten, and I think I'm just gonna stay right where I am." Mom smiled and nodded.

Well, as fate would have it, and despite my protests, I grew older. And then there came that time when I was about fifteen when all I wanted was to grow up and be a man. Men were cool. They could buy cars and drive motorcycles, and they had pretty girlfriends and wives. They didn't have to be in by 10 o'clock, and they could stay up late at night watching TV. And the ones I knew, although they certainly were not wealthy, always had money in their wallets.

A full-time mission grew me up in a hurry. Suddenly I was getting up at weird hours in the morning, walking down the streets of New York City or New Haven or Short Hills or Hartford, and knocking on the doors of people I didn't know from Adam. I was fielding hard questions from hostile ministers who knew more about Mormonism than I did, and I was wondering how a nice kid from Baton Rouge had managed to get himself into such a mess. I was washing my own clothes, cooking my own meals (or something like that), ironing my shirts, and writing checks for our rent and food. When I was ten I hadn't wanted to be a man, but now, whether I liked it or not, I was expected to act the part, even if

I didn't feel ready. Manhood had arrived. Ready or not, it had come.

As time went by, I stopped worrying about being a man and began to concern myself with a more specific issue: what *kind* of a man would I be? Would I be tough and macho, like John Wayne or Clark Gable? Tenderhearted and approachable like Robert Young (star of *Father Knows Best*) or Andy Griffith? A sports hero like Johnny Unitas or Arnold Palmer? Or would I be like some of the men in the Church I had encountered in the mission field? Would I ever be in a position to know the scriptures and teach the gospel with power and persuasion, like Harold B. Lee or Marion D. Hanks, general authorities who visited our mission regularly? Would I strive for the deep and profound spirituality of a Dewitt Paul, the patriarch in New Jersey, or Hugh West, the stake president in Connecticut? Would the day ever come when I would possess the dignity of Jay Eldredge, my first mission president, or would I ever adore and honor my wife like Harold Wilkinson, my second mission president?

Well, it's now been about forty years since I entered the Eastern States Mission, when I began to form a few opinions about what mattered most and when it became clear to me what kind of a man I wanted to be. My wife, Shauna, and I were married in 1971 and had six wonderful children—and now the number of grandchildren is on the rise. I have been privileged to work for the Church for over thirty years, most of that with the Church Educational System, and the rewards have been sweet indeed. Life has been good to me and mine, even with our heartaches and our challenges. God has been mindful of us and has never forsaken us, even in our lowest moments. Now, as I approach sixty years of age, I find myself, oddly, asking: What kind of a man have I become? And even more strangely: What kind of a man do I yet want to be?

Being a man in the twenty-first century is not easy. My guess is that each of us, whether we are nineteen or ninety, finds himself posing the questions: *What kind of a man am I? What kind of a man do I want to be?* And certainly more poignantly, *What kind of a man does my Heavenly Father and my Savior need me to be?* Things have changed in so very many ways from what I nostalgically and sentimentally call the "golden days" of the 1950s. Oh, there was crime and immorality back then, and indecency and corruption, to be sure. But it was a simpler time, a happier time, and evil had not spread its wings as broadly as they are spread today. Satan was alive and well in the days of Ozzie and Harriet and Beaver Cleaver, but the father of lies rules and reigns today on planet earth. It is, in fact, a great day for him, a day for the evil minions to celebrate their power. It is not unlike the time foreseen by Enoch the seer some five millennia ago: "And [Enoch] beheld Satan; and he had a great chain in his hand, and it veiled the whole face of the earth with darkness; and he looked up and laughed, and his angels rejoiced" (Moses 7:26).

Modern man has yielded to the harsh, the crude, the

vulgar, the profane, the immoral. Today's television sitcoms portray the father of the family (if there is one) very differently than Robert Young or Ozzie Nelson or Ward Cleaver. Rather than being a warm, wise, and loving friend to his wife and children, the father is typically depicted as a clumsy buffoon, an inane and even unnecessary appendage. In creating that caricature, producers and directors have done irreparable damage to the God-ordained image of what may be one of the most significant roles and offices in eternity—that of a father, that of a real man.

Thank God for holy scripture, which provides example after example of boys who became men who changed the world for good. Thank God for men of our own time who have refused to adorn themselves in the robes of mediocrity and compromise and worldliness, who are what they are and stand up for what they are. And thank God for spiritual leaders in our time who teach timeless and timely lessons; who have no desire whatsoever to be popular, only righteous; and who hold tenaciously to absolute truths amidst the shifting sands of secularity in a world rapidly plummeting toward ethical relativism.

As men of the covenant—as those who have come out of the world into the marvelous light of Christ—we have a job to do. Mormon pleaded with his son, Moroni, at a time when they observed with horror the disintegration of their own civilization: "And now, my beloved son, notwithstanding [the people's] hardness, let us labor diligently; for if we should cease to labor, we should be brought under condemnation; for *we have a labor to perform whilst in this tabernacle of clay, that we may conquer the enemy of all righteousness, and rest our souls in the kingdom of God*" (Moroni 9:6; emphasis added). They did, and we do. We have a world to awaken, a society to save, an ensign to erect, a message to deliver—a message containing glad tidings of great joy.

So many men in our world have been lulled into carnal security, have concluded that because they are not guilty of major violations of the law of the land or the law of God, all is well; some even within our own ranks fall into this category and have slipped ever so subtly into a spiritually comatose condition. Lehi's message, given some six centuries before the coming of the Messiah, seems very applicable to our day and time: "*O that ye would awake; awake from a deep sleep,* yea, even from the sleep of hell, and shake off the awful chains by which ye are bound. . . . Awake! and arise from the dust, and hear the words of a trembling parent. . . . *Arise from the dust, my sons, and be men,* and be determined in one mind and in one heart, united in all things, that ye may not come down into captivity. . . . *Awake, my sons; put on the armor of righteousness*" (2 Nephi 1:13, 14, 21, 23; emphasis added). Similarly, his son Jacob pleaded with the men of his day: "O my brethren, hearken unto my words; arouse the faculties of your souls; shake yourselves that ye may awake from the slumber of death" (Jacob 3:11).

Likewise, notice the sober warning and sublime promise

from King Benjamin: "O, all ye old men, and also ye young men, and you little children who can understand my words, . . . I pray that you should awake to a remembrance of the awful situation of those that have fallen into transgression. And moreover, I would desire that ye should consider on the blessed and happy state of those that keep the commandments of God. For behold, they are blessed in all things, both temporal and spiritual; and if they hold out faithful to the end they are received into heaven, that thereby they may dwell with God in a state of never-ending happiness. O remember, remember that these things are true; for the Lord God hath spoken it" (Mosiah 2:40–41).

As we take these warnings and promises to heart, we can partake of the magnificent power of the word of God that Alma the younger testified of. Speaking of how that power had transformed those taught by his father, he said: "Behold, [the Lord] *changed their hearts;* yea, he awakened them out of a deep sleep, and *they awoke unto God.* Behold, they were in the midst of darkness; nevertheless, their souls were illuminated by the light of the everlasting word" (Alma 5:7; emphasis added).

In short, we teach the gospel, we proclaim the message of salvation, and we call ourselves and others to repentance in order that people might be awakened to a sense of their duty toward God (see Alma 7:22).

A testimony of the gospel is a necessary but insufficient condition for salvation. Even the devils "believe and tremble"

(James 2:19). The importance of building upon one's testimony and thereafter becoming truly converted is dramatically illustrated in the life of Simon Peter. Peter was a humble man, a fisherman, when he was called by Jesus to the ministry. As a member of the meridian First Presidency, Peter was frequently alone with the Savior and was privy to many of the moving and pivotal spiritual experiences recorded in the New Testament (see Matthew 14:28–29; 17:1–9; 26:37; Mark 5:35–43). There is little doubt that Peter was a good man with solid desires, one who had a testimony of the divinity of Jesus of Nazareth. After Jesus had preached his powerful Bread of Life Sermon, in which he identified himself as the true Bread of Life and the Living Manna, many of the disciples were offended and "walked no more with him." Christ turned to the Twelve in a poignant moment and asked: "Will ye also go away?" Peter responded in deep sincerity and conviction, speaking for himself and the others of the Twelve: "Lord, to whom shall we go? thou hast the words of eternal life. And we believe and are sure that thou art that Christ, the Son of the living God" (John 6:66–69). At Caesarea Philippi some six months before the crucifixion, Jesus asked the Twelve: "Whom do men say that I the Son of man am?" Again answering for the Twelve, Peter said, "Thou art the Christ, the Son of the living God" (Matthew 16:16–19).

Although the New Testament attests to the fact that Peter had a testimony, it also affirms that he was weak—that he slipped and stumbled and fell. Not infrequently he was chastened by his Master for his shortsightedness and impulsiveness. Almost immediately after Peter's remarkable testimony at Caesarea Philippi, Jesus began to prepare his chosen Twelve for what lay ahead—his impending arrest, passion, and death. "Then Peter took him, and began to rebuke him, saying, Be it far from thee, Lord: this shall not be unto thee. But [Jesus] turned, and said unto Peter, Get thee behind me, Satan: thou art an offence unto me; for thou savourest not the things that be of God, but those that be of men" (Matthew 16:21-23). Here we see that Peter, the rock or seer stone (JST John 1:42), had become a stumbling block. And of course there was the most classic of Peter's blunders—when he denied knowing Christ on three separate occasions on the night the Savior was arrested (Matthew 26:69-74).

How could one who had a testimony fall short so often? How could one who knew as Peter knew slip as often as Peter did, even to the point of an outright denial? The answer to such questions seems to lie in a conversation between Jesus and Peter at the Last Supper. Jesus said: "Simon, Simon, behold, Satan hath desired to have you, that he may sift you as wheat: But I have prayed for thee, that thy faith fail not: and *when thou art converted, strengthen thy brethren*" (Luke 22:31-32; emphasis added). Though Peter had a testimony, he was not fully converted. Inasmuch as the full power and gifts of the Holy Ghost were not given until the day of Pentecost, Peter had enjoyed only flashes of inspiration. After the resurrection of the Lord and after Pentecost and the accompanying baptism by fire, Peter and the Twelve would walk in a new light. One needs only to read the opening chapters of the Acts of the Apostles to witness a transformation in the man Peter. He is bold and certain and solid in his ministry—a permanent and indelible impression had been planted, for the Spirit had made Peter into a new creature in Christ.

As Peter and John walked through the Gate Beautiful on the way to the temple (as recorded in Acts 3), they passed a lame man who begged alms daily. President Harold B. Lee described this touching scene: "Here was one who had never walked, impotent from his birth, begging alms of all who approached the gate. And as Peter and John approached, he held out his hand expectantly, asking for alms. Peter, speaking for this pair of missionaries—Church authorities—said, 'Look on us.' And, of course, that heightened his expectation. 'Then Peter said, Silver and gold have I none; but such as I have give I thee: In the name of Jesus Christ of Nazareth rise up and walk' (Acts 3:4, 6)."

President Lee continued: "Will you see that picture now of that noble soul, that chiefest of the apostles, perhaps with his arms around the shoulders of this man, and saying, 'Now, my good man, have courage, I will take a few steps with you. Let's walk together, and I assure you that you can walk, because you have received a blessing by the power and authority that God has given us as men, his servants.' Then the man leaped with joy."

Through the cultivation of the gift of the Holy Ghost, Peter was born again, converted, turned wholly to Christ and to His righteousness. Peter could now strengthen his brothers and sisters. *"You cannot lift another soul,"* President Lee added, *"until you are standing on higher ground than he is. You must be sure, if you would rescue the man, that you yourself are setting the example of what you would have him be. You cannot light a fire in another soul unless it is burning in your own soul"* (Conference Report, April 1973, 178; emphasis added). Truly, "one is converted when he sees with his eyes what he ought to see; when he hears with his ears what he ought to hear; and when he understands with his heart what he ought to understand. And what he ought to see, hear, and understand is truth—eternal truth—and then practice it. That is conversion. . . .

"When we understand more than we know with our minds, when we understand with our hearts, then we know that the Spirit of the Lord is working upon us" (Lee, *Stand Ye in Holy Places*, 92).

President Lee called upon us to stand on higher ground, to place ourselves in a position to lift and liberate and lighten the burdens of others, to help them see things from an elevated perspective, to see with new eyes and feel with a new heart. "This journey to higher ground," Elder Joseph B. Wirthlin explained, "is the pathway of discipleship to the Lord Jesus Christ. It is a journey that will ultimately lead us to exaltation with our families in the presence of the Father and the Son. Consequently, our journey to higher ground must include the house of the Lord. As we come unto Christ and journey to higher ground, we will desire to spend more time in His temples, because the temples represent higher ground, sacred ground.

"In every age we are faced with a choice. We can trust in our own strength, or we can journey to higher ground and come unto Christ. Each choice has a consequence. Each consequence, a destination" (Conference Report, October 2005, 18).

You and I are not here on earth at this time by chance. We are here as a part of a grand plan of salvation, during an era in earth's history when the forces of the enemy are combined (see D&C 38:12). But it is also a time when God has chosen to restore his holy priesthood through modern prophets and engage the forbidding enemies of the kingdom—attacks on marriage and the family, immorality, violence, insensitivity, and preoccupation and distraction—through the weak and the simple, that is, through those President Joseph F. Smith called "soldiers of the Cross" (*Gospel Doctrine*, 91). "Wherefore, I call upon the weak things of the world, those who are unlearned and despised, to thrash the nations by the power of my Spirit; And their arm shall be my arm, and I will be their shield and their buckler; and I will gird up their loins, and they shall fight manfully for me; . . . and by the fire of mine indignation will I preserve them" (D&C 35:13; compare 1:19, 23).

I believe the message in the hymn "Rise Up, O Men of God" (*Hymns,* no. 324) is a plea, a call, a divine invitation for us to rise above the telestial tinsel of our time; to deny ourselves of ungodliness and clothe ourselves in the mantle of holiness; to reach and stretch and grasp for that spiritual direction and sacred empowerment promised to the Lord's agents, to those charged to act in the name of our Principal, Jesus Christ; and to point the way to salvation and deliverance and peace in a world that finds itself enshrouded in darkness, a world that yearns for spiritual leadership. Nephi prophesied of a time when the power of the Lamb of God "descended upon the saints of the church of the Lamb, and upon the covenant people of the Lord, who were scattered upon all the face of the earth; and they were armed with righteousness and with the power of God in great glory" (1 Nephi 14:14). That day and the time are upon us. Let us step forward and respond enthusiastically to the call.

POINTS TO PONDER

1. What does it mean to "grow up unto the Lord" (Helaman 3:21)?

2. How often do I think about what kind of man I want to be? How often do I think about what others will remember most about me? What kind of priesthood legacy am I leaving?

3. The Prophet Lehi pleaded with his sons repeatedly to "Awake! and arise from the dust" (2 Nephi 1:14). In what

ways do I need to wake up? How is it that I have been called to arise from the dust? (see D&C 113:7–10).

4. Peter was counseled by the Master at the Last Supper to become converted and then to strengthen his brethren (Luke 22:31–32). In what areas of my life do I need to undergo a conversion, a mighty change? How can my conversion then be used to lift and bless the lives of my brethren and sisters?

HAVE DONE WITH
LESSER THINGS

DURING THE SUMMER OF 1975 I was asked to work with the leaders of the curriculum division of the Church Educational System in downtown Salt Lake City. Our young family was living in West Jordan, Utah, at the time in our first purchased home. I discovered that an early-morning city bus would pick me up just in front of our home and drop me off near the Church Office Building, and so I began taking the bus to work regularly. Since the ride took a little less than an hour, I decided to use the time wisely and read. Someone had recommended a particular book on time management, and so I purchased a copy and began to devour it.

The author asked readers to sit down and make a list of goals—one-month, one-year, five-year, ten-year, and lifetime goals, which I did. He then taught readers how to prioritize our activities into A, B, and C tasks, A being the most critical and C being good but not vital. The next step: write down all of the activities of the last week and then prioritize the activities into A, B, and C. He then asked this horrible, unsettling, and guilt-producing question: "Now, how much of your time last week was spent on A tasks?" It didn't take an astrophysicist to compute the results. In my heart of hearts it was clear that drawing closer to my Heavenly Father, serving the people about me, and growing in gospel scholarship—along with devoting as much time as I could to my wife, children, and extended family—were the actions that had long-term, even eternal implications. Yet in reality I had spent the bulk of my time the previous week shuffling from one C activity to another. I could talk the talk, to be sure, but I wasn't walking the walk. My eternal values were not being reflected in my daily doings.

It is startling how easy it is in today's busy and complex world to get caught up in the thick of thin things, to become prey to the less important. Means begin to occupy us more than ends. Making a living, being included in the best social circles, providing the family with nice cars, lovely clothes, or extravagant travel opportunities—these may make life enjoyable and comfortable, but they are not the stuff out of which eternal happiness is made. Life is a mission and not a career.

People matter more than things. People matter more than schedules and timetables and products. God and Christ work full time in the business of people, and surely that primary labor contributes in great measure to their fulness of joy. Sometimes when the most important things tend to get crowded out by the least important, the Lord finds a way to jerk us back to reality and focus us on fundamentals. Occasionally it comes through the staggering confrontation with death, the stark realization that we are here on earth for only a brief season. Often it comes through what we call tragedy—an injury, a crippling disease, a terrible trauma. And once in a while it comes through incidents much less dramatic but direct.

Only a few years into our marriage I sat on the floor in front of a small bookcase in the dining room of our tiny two-bedroom apartment. I was immersed in reading and referencing and marking; I was in the process of preparing a book for publication. Deadlines were crowding in on me. Interestingly (and ironically), I was perusing President David O. McKay's book, *Gospel Ideals*, when Angie, my oldest daughter, then just over two years old, walked over to me and asked me to join her, our one-year old, and my wife, Shauna, in some games they were playing on the floor about twenty feet away. I responded to Angie that I was very busy and couldn't make it. Within three minutes David crawled over and asked: "Dad, you come play?" I called out to my wife at that point: "Shauna, can't you see that what I am doing is important? Could you please keep these children out of my hair until I finish?" (I had hair then!)

I dove back into my research. But then I felt my attention being drawn back to the threesome, almost as if I were being physically turned around. I looked into three sets of eyes, and what I saw was not very settling—there was hurt and, in Shauna's eyes, at least, a bit of disappointed frustration. And then a voice came into my mind. Whether it was the voice of the Holy Ghost or the voice of conscience, I don't know: it was nevertheless an inner awareness of my duty. It stated simply but boldly: "Brother, behold the plan of salvation!" In that brief instant there came a cluster of feelings—feelings of perspective, for in a flash I saw and felt things as they really were; feelings of overwhelming love for a trusting wife and adorable children; and yes, feelings of guilt for neglecting the most important mortals in my life. A rapidly repentant father crawled over to his family and became involved in things that really matter.

In the years since that experience, I have reflected again and again on what I felt that evening. Maybe it was the consuming love for my family, coupled with a cold slap in the face, that awakened me momentarily. Other things over the years have served a like function. Shauna has gotten my attention occasionally when I chose to bury myself in a book and ignore the family. She has said simply: "Bob, if you're not careful, you may grow up to be a very intelligent ministering angel!" That works too! Truly, as Elder M. Russell Ballard has reminded us, "What matters most is what lasts longest, and our families are for eternity" (Conference Report, October 2005, 46).

One of the really ironic things I have noticed in my own life is our frequent unwillingness to be as patient and forgiving with family members as we are with friends, associates, or even strangers. Most of us wouldn't consider publicly insulting a colleague or belittling an acquaintance or slipping into the silent treatment with co-workers at church. But we so often do those very things to those who matter most to us. Because we desperately want our little ones to be ever so much better than we were, we tend to be impatient with their lack of progress, irritated at their mistakes in judgment, and downright angry about their failings. I have far too often caught myself shaking my head and wondering when the spirit of life and good judgment would descend upon my teenagers, especially when I found that their choices were not as wise as I would have preferred. If, however, the Lord had wanted to put a forty-year-old head on the shoulders of a sixteen-year-old young person, I suppose he would have done so; instead, he almost always attaches the head (and heart and emotions and hormones) of a sixteen year old to a sixteen year old.

How often do we find ourselves, though well-intentioned, driven by the tyranny of the urgent? More than once my friend and mentor, Robert J. Matthews, said to me, "Robert L., be careful not to spend your life laboring in secondary causes." That's a haunting warning. It reminds me of the chastening words of Samuel the Lamanite to the wayward Nephites: "But behold," he said, "your days of probation are past; ye have procrastinated the day of your salvation until it is everlastingly too late, and your destruction is made sure;

yea, for ye have sought all the days of your lives for that which ye could not obtain; and ye have sought for happiness in doing iniquity, which thing is contrary to the nature of that righteousness which is in our great and Eternal Head" (Helaman 13:38).

What a tragedy it would be to spend our days climbing a ladder, only to realize as we reached the top that all the while the ladder had been leaning against the wrong wall! We cannot expect to find delight with our companion in our golden years or especially in eternity if our mortal investments in family matters are minimal or missing. We cannot expect to enjoy the sweet association of the Spirit in our mature years if we have not sought to cultivate that Spirit and its gifts in the moments and hours and months leading up to that time. The Law of the Harvest (Galatians 6:7–8) is irrevocable. The Law of Restoration (Alma 41) is real.

Elder Jeffrey R. Holland once described a painful situation in his own family. "Early in our married life my young family and I were laboring through graduate school at a university in New England. Pat was the Relief Society president in our ward, and I was serving in our stake presidency. I was going to school full-time and teaching half-time. We had two small children then, with little money and lots of pressures. In fact, our life was about like yours.

"One evening I came home from long hours at school, feeling the proverbial weight of the world on my shoulders.

Everything seemed to be especially demanding and discouraging and dark. I wondered if the dawn would ever come. Then, as I walked into our small student apartment, there was an unusual silence in the room.

"'What's the trouble?' I asked. 'Matthew has something he wants to tell you,' Pat said. 'Matt, what do you have to tell me?' He was quietly playing with his toys in the corner of the room, trying very hard not to hear me. 'Matt,' I said a little louder, 'do you have something to tell me?'

"He stopped playing, but for a moment didn't look up. Then these two enormous, tear-filled brown eyes turned toward me, and with the pain only a five-year-old can know, he said, 'I didn't mind Mommy tonight, and I spoke back to her.' With that he burst into tears, and his entire little body shook with grief. A childish indiscretion had been noted, a painful confession had been offered, the growth of a five-year-old was continuing, and loving reconciliation could have been wonderfully underway.

"Everything might have been just terrific—except for me. If you can imagine such an idiotic thing, I lost my temper. It wasn't that I lost it with Matt—it was with a hundred and one other things on my mind; but he didn't know that, and I wasn't disciplined enough to admit it. He got the whole load of bricks.

"I told him how disappointed I was and how much more I thought I could have expected from him. I sounded like the parental pygmy I was. Then I did what I had never done before in his life—I told him that he was to go straight to bed and that I would not be in to say his prayers with him or to tell him a bedtime story. Muffling his sobs, he obediently went to his bedside, where he knelt—alone—to say his prayers. Then he stained his little pillow with tears his father should have been wiping away.

"If you think the silence upon my arrival was heavy, you should have felt it now. Pat did not say a word. She didn't have to. I felt terrible!

"Later, as we knelt by our own bed, my feeble prayer for blessings upon my family fell back on my ears with a horrible, hollow ring. I wanted to get up off my knees right then and go to Matt and ask his forgiveness, but he was long since peacefully asleep.

"*My* relief was not so soon coming; but finally I fell asleep and began to dream, which I seldom do. I dreamed Matt and I were packing two cars for a move. For some reason his mother and baby sister were not present. As we finished I turned to him and said, 'Okay, Matt, you drive one car and I'll drive the other.'

"This five-year-old very obediently crawled up on the seat and tried to grasp the massive steering wheel. I walked over to the other car and started the motor. As I began to pull away, I looked to see how my son was doing. He was trying— oh, how he was trying. He tried to reach the pedals, but he couldn't. He was also turning knobs and pushing buttons, trying to start the motor. He could scarcely be seen over the dashboard, but there staring out at me again were those same immense, tear-filled, beautiful brown eyes. As I pulled away, he cried out, 'Daddy, don't leave me. I don't know how to do it. I am too little.' And I drove away.

"A short time later, driving down that desert road in my dream, I suddenly realized in one stark, horrifying moment what I had done. I slammed my car to a stop, threw open the door, and started to run as fast as I could. I left car, keys, belongings, and all—and I ran. The pavement was so hot it burned my feet, and tears blinded my straining effort to see this child somewhere on the horizon. I kept running, praying, pleading to be forgiven and to find my boy safe and secure.

"As I rounded a curve nearly ready to drop from physical and emotional exhaustion, I saw the unfamiliar car I had left Matt to drive. It was pulled carefully off to the side of the road, and he was laughing and playing nearby. An older man was with him, playing and responding to his games. Matt saw me and cried out something like, 'Hi, Dad. We're having fun.' Obviously he had already forgiven and forgotten my terrible transgression against him.

"But I dreaded the older man's gaze, which followed my every move. I tried to say 'Thank you,' but his eyes were filled with sorrow and disappointment. I muttered an awkward apology and the stranger said simply, 'You should not have left him alone to do this difficult thing. It would not have been asked of you.'

"With that, the dream ended, and I shot upright in bed. *My* pillow was now stained, whether with perspiration or tears I do not know. I threw off the covers and ran to the little metal camp cot that was my son's bed. There on my knees and through my tears I cradled him in my arms and spoke to him while he slept. I told him that every dad makes mistakes but that they don't mean to. I told him it wasn't his fault I had had a bad day. I told him that when boys are five or fifteen, dads sometimes forget and think they are fifty. I told him that I wanted him to be a small boy for a long, long time, because all too soon he would grow up and be a man and wouldn't be playing on the floor with his toys when I came home. I told him that I loved him and his mother and his sister more than anything in the world and that whatever challenges we had in life we would face them together. I told him that never again would I withhold my affection or my forgiveness from him, and never, I prayed, would he withhold them from me. I told him I was honored to be his father and that I would try with all my heart to be worthy of such a great responsibility" (Conference Report, April 1983, 52–53; emphasis in original).

It was Jesus who taught us in the Sermon on the Mount: "Lay not up for yourselves treasures upon earth, where moth and rust doth corrupt, and where thieves break through and steal: but lay up for yourselves treasures in heaven, where neither moth nor rust doth corrupt, and where thieves do not break through nor steal: For *where your treasure is, there will your heart be also*" (Matthew 6:19–21; emphasis added). If I begin to be conformed to the values of this ephemeral world, if my treasures take the form of automobiles, the size of my home, sports equipment, portfolios, country clubs, and leisure time, then my heart will begin to yearn for more and more of such things. Such things are like "slippery riches": they will not and cannot satisfy. If, on the other hand, my living sacrifice consists of placing the animal within me on the altar, if my treasures take the form of integrity, decency, kindness, sensitivity, character, and people—especially those closest to me—then my mind and my heart will begin to be transformed by the Master; I will have gained "the mind of Christ" (1 Corinthians 2:16; see also Romans 12:1–2). I will come to see things as they really are, covet earnestly the best gifts, and seek to spend my time and energies in primary causes.

Many years ago President Boyd K. Packer spoke to the youth: "Some day—some day soon for some of you—you are going to have the marvelous experience of learning to love someone else more than you love yourself. This is a crowning achievement in life, yet countless thousands live out there in this world and do not achieve this experience. It does not come, I think, in a courtship or even on a honeymoon; but it is a reward for building this little [family] kingdom. Someday when you hold a little boy or a little girl in your arms and know that he belongs to you, this experience may come to you.

"I recall on one occasion, when I was returning from seminary to my home for lunch, that as I drove in my wife met me in the driveway. I could tell by the expression on her face that something was wrong. 'Cliff has been killed,' she said. 'They want you to come over.' As I hastened around the corner to where Cliff lived with his wife and four sons and his little daughter, I saw Cliff lying in the middle of the highway with a blanket over him. The ambulance was just pulling away with little Colleen. Cliff had been on his way out to the farm and had stopped to cross the street to take little Colleen to her mother who waited on the opposite curb. But the child, as children will, broke from her father's hand and slipped into the street. A large truck was coming. Cliff jumped from the curb and pushed his little daughter from the path of the truck—but he wasn't soon enough.

"A few days later I had the responsibility of talking at the funeral of Cliff and little Colleen. Someone said, 'What a terrible waste. Certainly he ought to have stayed on the curb. He knew the child might have died. But he had four sons and a wife to provide for. What a pathetic waste!' And I estimated that that individual never had had the experience of loving someone more than he loved himself.

"To you who are young, this experience of loving someone more than you love yourself can come, insofar as I know, only through the exercise of the power of creation. Through it you become really Christian, and you know, as few others know, what the word 'Father' means when it is spoken of in the scriptures; and you feel some of the love and concern that he has for us, and you may experience some of the remorse and sorrow that must be his if we fail to accept all that is beautiful and praiseworthy and of good report in this world" (Address, 15 July 1958).

The men of God are called upon to "have done with lesser things." Lesser things do not satisfy. They do not fill the hunger of the human soul. They do not bring peace and rest. Lesser things do not build the family unit, bring harmony into the home, or fortify relationships that are intended to be everlasting. Lesser things do not enhance personal spirituality. They do not cause us to want to enter the divine presence. They do not bring comfort in moments of crisis. The Apostle Paul, in writing to the saints at Philippi, looked back on his life with a perspective born of the Spirit. He described his attention to rabbinic detail before his conversion on the road to Damascus as follows: "Circumcised the eighth day, of the stock of Israel, of the tribe of Benjamin, an Hebrew of the Hebrews; as touching the law. A Pharisee; concerning zeal, persecuting the church; touching the righteousness which is in the law, blameless."

In other words, Paul was as "righteous" and filled with Jewish "piety" as one could possibly be; there was no stone unturned in his life, no jot or tittle out of place. But then Christ entered in. The Savior came into his life and turned it upside down. His worldview was shattered, his goals tarnished, and his ambitions revealed for what they were, namely, "lesser things." Notice what follows: "But what things were gain to me, those I counted loss for Christ." In other words, his value system was reversed. The things that had mattered most now mattered least. The things he once despised and attacked he now came to treasure and adore. "Yea doubtless, and *I count all things but loss for the excellency of the knowledge of Christ Jesus my Lord: for whom I have suffered the loss of all things,* and do count them but dung, that I may win Christ, and be found in him, not having mine own righteousness, which is of the law, but that which is through the faith of Christ, the righteousness which is of God by faith: *that I may know him,* and the power of his resurrection, and the fellowship of his sufferings" (Philippians 3:7–10; emphasis added).

Obviously how we think and what we think about will determine our future, even our destiny. God and his chosen servants have entreated the men of the Church, those called out of the world, to think eternally as they act daily. When we think eternal thoughts, our actions will be lasting and worthwhile. When we think eternally, our impact on our homes and our society will be permanent. When we think eternally, the things that matter most will never be sacrificed to the things that matter least. And when we view our lives from an eternal vantage point, we will recognize that we are indeed agents on the Lord's errand; we will then do things his way (D&C 64:29).

POINTS TO PONDER

1. It has often been said that we become prey to the "tyranny of the urgent." To what extent am I driven more by the pressing than the eternal?

2. Reflect on the past week and ask: What are some instances in which the most important matters of my life took a back seat to matters of lesser worth?

3. If my wife or children were asked what the most important things in their husband's or father's life are, how would they answer?

4. What immediately comes to my mind when I am asked to "have done with lesser things?" What are some lesser things in my life that seem to monopolize my time and energies?

GIVING HEART AND SOUL

MY FATHER PASSED AWAY in March of 1988 at the young age of sixty-one (it now seems very, very young). He had been sickly for the final years of his life and had suffered endlessly from the spreading effects of diabetes. We as a family had prayed him through several bouts with death and had pleaded earnestly with the Lord to allow him to stay with us a little longer. In each case, as Shauna, the children, and I had knelt and prayed for Paw Paw Millet's life, the quiet but sweet assurance had come that our prayers had been heard and acknowledged, that Dad would be allowed to remain in mortality for a season.

I remember the day Dad phoned me and said, "Well, son, I suppose you ought to hop a plane and get down here in a hurry." I asked why. He said: "The doctor has given me a few days to live. I'm dying from sclerosis of the liver. What do you think about that?" he asked. "I'm dying from a drinking man's disease, and I've never enjoyed the benefits!" We both laughed. Dad was not afraid of death. In fact, he and I had spoken on many, many occasions of the postmortal spirit world, and he had commented more than once how eager he was to see his mother and father again and how excited he was to have some of our questions about the life beyond answered. We entered into a pact that whichever one of us went first through the veil of death would return and tell the other one all about it. There must be rules there, just as there are here, for even though Dad's words have been heard and his influence felt powerfully by members of my family, he hasn't yet returned to deliver the goods.

Death comes in many ways. My maternal grandmother slipped into eternity in an instant, suddenly, as she and grandpa were watching a football game. While she was not a Latter-day Saint, she was a saintly woman who loved God, loved her family, and loved and served his children. I have felt fortunate that I was able to spend Dad's last hours with him. I flew down to Baton Rouge, rented a car, and drove to their home, arriving about 10:30 P.M. the evening after he had phoned me. We sat in the living room for several hours talking about old times, about life here and now, and about the life that lay ahead for him. I helped put him in bed, and he asked me to sit beside him. I tried my darndest to tell him how proud I was of him, how much he had meant to so many people in business, in the community, and especially in the Church. I tried to thank him for all that he had taught me through the years by example—integrity and honesty and hard work and charity and single-minded dedication to the cause of the Master. But Dad kept changing the subject; he didn't want to talk about himself. He said he wanted to discuss things that matter most. He knew, and I knew, that a chapter in his eternal journey was coming to a close. We then spoke at length about home and family and temples and covenants and sealings and eternal life. We expressed our love to each other and brought to an end, at least for a short season, a sweet association, one that I look forward to resuming even more than I can say.

I knew then that I would miss him, that our family, especially my mother, would mourn his loss, and that it would be impossible to completely fill the void of his passing. And yet there was no doubt whatsoever, in his heart or mine, that Albert Louis Millet would continue to live, that he was about to be transferred to another field of labor. I was totally at peace during those tender moments, and that consummate assurance continued through his death and funeral. It continues to this day, after two decades. It is a peace born of perspective, a peace undergirded by the restored doctrine of life beyond the grave. It is a peace that derives from that Spirit which confirms that what my father had taught me through the years relative to life after death was indeed true.

I think often of those sacred hours with my beloved earthly father. They teach me a great deal about living and dying, about what I ought to be doing in between those two singular events, about how I ought to spend my time and energies, and about what really brings satisfaction to the soul here and hereafter. We are sent to earth, our second estate, to be proven, "to see if [we] will do all things whatsoever the Lord [our] God shall command [us]." We have been taught further that "they who keep their second estate shall have glory added upon their heads for ever and ever" (Abraham 3:25, 26). And how do we "keep" our second estate? We come to discover or rediscover God our Eternal Father and his plan of salvation that has been in place from the foundation of the world. We come to recognize our weakness and our weaknesses, to acknowledge our sinfulness and need for divine deliverance from sin and death; that is, we rejoice in the majestic mission and ministry of Jesus the Christ, our Lord and Redeemer. We learn to walk by faith, to search the scriptures, to listen to the prophets, to attend to the still small voice within us—by these means we come to sense who we are and Whose we are. By these means we come to know what things matter and what things don't, what endeavors in life are primary and what engagements are secondary.

Most of us spend many, many years trying to do things on our own. We believe in God, to be sure. We know of the availability of the precious grace and tender mercies of Jesus. And yet our hearts tend to cry out (even if we never utter the words), "I can handle it!" The fact is, I cannot handle it; neither can you. No one can "handle" life without help, particularly heavenly help. There comes that moment when it dawns upon us—and a singular moment it is—when we admit to the fact that our omnipotent, omniscient, and omni-loving God can do far more with our lives than we can. Humility ushers us into the realm of submission and surrender. And, ironically, submission and unconditional surrender to the true Captain of our souls lead eventually to victory. "Thanks be to God," Paul exulted, "[who] giveth us the victory through our Lord Jesus Christ" (1 Corinthians 15:57). In short, there is peace, there is rest, there is victory associated with doing things God's way, through "giving heart and soul" to our Lord and inviting his active participation and direction in our lives.

Over forty years ago I sat in the home of a friend a few hours before I was to leave Salt Lake City for a full-time mission to the Eastern States. This friend's powerful missionary example in the Gulf States Mission had helped me decide to serve a mission. "Gary," I asked, "what could you say to help me be a successful missionary?" He didn't even hesitate: "You keep an eye single to the glory of God, and you'll be successful." I thanked him for his counsel, but inwardly I felt cheated. Surely, I thought, there was something more specific that could make me a better finder, teacher, and baptizer. I was in the mission field only two days before the import of his advice became evident. Indeed, he could not have hit the mark more directly. Over the years since, I have discovered how vital this principle is in the work of the kingdom. The task of the disciple of Christ is to deny oneself, to seek the way of the Master, to be willing to forsake the manmade and the material, and to pursue with steadfastness the divine and the everlasting. For the disciple, it is the kingdom of God or nothing! Indeed, as a wise cleric of centuries past proclaimed, If you have not chosen the kingdom of God first, it will make little difference what you have chosen instead.

"Then one of them, which was a lawyer, asked [Jesus] a question, tempting him, and saying, Master, which is the great commandment in the law? Jesus said unto him, Thou shalt love the Lord thy God with all thy heart, and with all thy soul, and with all thy mind. This is the first and great commandment. And the second is like unto it, Thou shalt love thy neighbor as thyself. On these two commandments hang all the law and the prophets" (Matthew 22:35–40). A modern revelation sets forth the same high standard that serves as a divine distillation of what God expects of you and me: "Thou shalt love the Lord thy God with all thy heart, with all thy might, mind, and strength; and in the name of Jesus Christ thou shalt serve him. Thou shalt love thy neighbor as thyself" (D&C 59:5–6). While I know that we have heard these scriptural passages hundreds of times, let's take a few moments and reflect on their profundity. To love God with all our heart is to love him from the very core of our being, the seat of our emotions. To love God with all our might is to do so with all our strength, our energy, and our physical capacity. To love God with all our soul is to love him with body and spirit, with the whole of us.

I am particularly fascinated with what it means to love God with all our mind. Maybe it's because I have spent my professional life as a religious educator, but I sincerely believe Latter-day Saints, and especially those called and charged to bear the holy priesthood, should love our Heavenly Father and his Son with our minds more than we do. To love God with our minds is to think upon him, to seek to better comprehend his person and his nature, to strive to grasp those verities that are termed the mysteries of godliness (see 1 Timothy 3:16; D&C 19:10)—things that can be understood only by the power of the Holy Spirit.

To love God with our minds is to become more serious students of holy scripture, to yearn to become gospel scholars, to find sheer delight in the discovery of new truths and new applications of scriptural passages. To love God with all our minds is to develop and maintain a curiosity about life and the cosmos, to read broadly, to learn from others who know more than we do, to open ourselves to deeper understandings, to never be static or sterile or fossilized in our faith and learning. In short, to love God with all our minds is to consecrate our thinking, reasoning, and mental capacities to Him who knows all things, to stand ready, as Peter commissioned us, to provide a reason for the hope within us (1 Peter 3:15), to possess an understanding of the message of salvation that is as satisfying to the mind as it is settling and soothing to the heart, to not only know the gospel is true, but to know the gospel.

Too many people in our day are seeking to fulfill the second great commandment—to love our neighbors as ourselves—while giving but passing attention to the first. And this cannot be done. We cannot truly love and serve our fellow men and women, at least in the manner Deity has designed, unless we first learn to love God. President Ezra Taft Benson asked: "Why did God put the first commandment first? Because He knew that if we truly loved Him we would want to keep all of His other commandments. . . .

"We must put God in the forefront of everything else in our lives. He must come first, just as He declares in the first of his Ten Commandments: 'Thou shalt have no other gods before me' (Exodus 20:3).

"When we put God first, all other things fall into their proper place or drop out of our lives. Our love of the Lord will govern the claims for our affection, the demands on our time, the interests we pursue, and the order of our priorities.

"We should put God ahead of *everyone else* in our lives" (Conference Report, April 1988, 3; emphasis in original).

To give heart and soul to serve our Heavenly King is to decide as priesthood holders that God and the things of God really do come first; that while it is food for the ego to be thought important in business, it is manna to the soul to have family and members of the household of faith recognize us as righteous and true; that while it brings self-satisfaction to be in demand, it is a marvelous blessing for our priesthood leaders to know that we are dependable and steady; and that while it is nice to achieve financial security, it is even nicer to have acquired eternal security. The question is frequently asked: "What comes first, Church or family?" Well, doesn't the kingdom lead out? No, isn't the family the most important unit in time and eternity? The fact is, God comes first, and if we seek his will, he will make known to us what, in that specific instance, comes second.

I rather think on the day of judgment it will matter precious little to our Father in Heaven *where* we have served in the Church—whether as a scoutmaster, a clerk, a Primary teacher, or a building supervisor. The real issue will be *how* we served. Were we there on time? Did we prepare ourselves properly to make a difference? Did we pray earnestly for guidance and direction, as well as for the spirit of our calling? Did we work in harmony and love with those associated most closely with us? Did we sustain and uphold our leaders?

I can still remember as a college student transferring to Brigham Young University and being introduced on the Sabbath to this strange and unusual thing called a BYU ward. The bishopric of a student or singles ward feel quite overwhelmed at the start of a new year, especially as they are required to re-staff almost the entire ward. Our bishop sustained scores of people that first Sunday and then took a little longer to announce the call of a young woman.

He said, in essence: "Last year Sarah Jackson [not her real name] was called to serve as an assistant sacrament coordinator; her job was to see to it that the cloth that covers the sacramental trays was always beautifully white and pressed. Sarah did her job magnificently. We never needed to worry about the sacrament cloth. She magnified her calling as well as anyone we have ever worked with. In that spirit, we present to you, for your sustaining vote, the name of Sarah Jackson to serve as our ward Relief Society president."

I was deeply moved by the bishop's words, and there echoed in my mind the Savior's commendation to those in the parable of the talents who had been faithful in magnifying their talents: "Well done, thou good and faithful servant: thou hast been faithful over a few things, I will make thee ruler over many things: enter thou into the joy of thy Lord" (Matthew 25:21, 23).

We do not do our duty in the Church with the hope of being called to something greater. God knows where we are. He knows what the ward or stake needs. And he knows what you or I need at a given time. Rather, we do our duty because we know that we are a part of a greater whole and that no one aspect, no one part of the body of Christ, is any greater than the other. "Therefore, let every man stand in his own office, and labor in his own calling; and let not the head say unto the feet it hath no need of the feet; for without the feet how shall the body be able to stand? Also the body hath need of every member, that all may be edified together, that the system may be kept perfect" (D&C 84:109–10). Having served twice now as a bishop, in four stake presidencies, and as a stake president, I say without reservation that I would trade charisma for steadiness any day; I would trade talent and ability any time for dependability. The Lord desperately needs people who are steadfast and immovable, simple Saints who go about the work of the kingdom with little or no concern about who notices or how much praise or notoriety follows.

One doesn't need to be a bishop or high priest group leader or elders quorum president to help move the kingdom of God forward. A man can be a committed and loving and caring home teacher and do far more good than he has any idea. It is a privilege, a consummate privilege to have the Melchizedek Priesthood conferred upon us. Through that conferral, and the ordination to office that accompanies it, comes an assignment, a built-in assignment, an assignment to which one does not need to be set apart, a sacred assignment to minister to others as a home teacher—a priesthood representative, an under-shepherd in a role that is clearly "dear to the heart of the Shepherd" (*Hymns,* no. 221).

I have witnessed miracles occur through the quiet but faithful labors of home teachers. I have witnessed many less-active members taught and loved and fellowshipped back into the sheepfold. I have seen those burdened almost beyond despair lifted and strengthened and reoriented by attentive and inspired home teachers who recognized that their calling involved more than a monthly visit for the record. At a time when life was extremely busy and hectic for me—when I was working on my doctoral degree, was the bishop of our ward, was the institute director and supervisor of five stakes of seminary—and when the pressure was heavy upon Shauna's shoulders to attend to family matters while her husband was trying to finish school, we were blessed with honorable and focused home teachers.

I remember very well that Mark Peddie asked us each month in his regular visit (during President Kimball's administration) whether we had started to plant our garden. Each month I timidly replied that we hadn't yet planted our tomatoes and cucumbers and squash but planned to do so soon. I came home from a long day one afternoon only to find that a large plot of ground in our backyard had been tilled, rocks and weeds had been discarded, and a beautiful garden had been planted for us. Now that's what faithful home teachers do! On a later occasion, one of us (I'm sure it must have been Shauna) backed out of the driveway and ran over our mailbox. Being preoccupied with other things, I never seemed to find a block of time to purchase a new one and install it. Then one day I came home to find a brand-new and attractive mailbox in front of our home. The home teachers had dropped by, recognized the need, and acted. They seldom if ever asked, "What can we do for you?" Instead, they were observant, attentive, sensitive, and involved in our lives. They were giving heart and soul to serve their Heavenly King through serving our Heavenly King's children (see Matthew 25:40; Mosiah 2:17).

I have also learned that while home teaching visits need to be regular and consistent and warm and friendly, there are times when chats about the weather and the upcoming football season just don't cut it. Some thirty-five years ago I was assigned to visit a family that was less active, a home where tragedy had struck several years before, taking two of their little ones in death. Obviously both mom and dad were devastated, heartbroken, and, by the time I got to know them, bitter. They were mad at God, mad at life, mad at the Church. They wanted to know why, *why* a loving Heavenly Father would permit such a hideous and unloving thing to shatter their world. I spent the first six or seven visits trying to encourage them to turn off the TV when we came, simply trying to build a friendship and an atmosphere of trust and goodwill. Eventually they began to talk with us and even began to listen occasionally.

One month as my companion and I knelt to pray before leaving to visit them, I had the strongest and most forceful feeling come over me that it was time to challenge them to leave the past alone and move forward. I didn't know at that moment what such a challenge would entail, but I sensed that this home teaching visit would be very different from those of the past. We knocked at the door, the family invited us in, and we caught up on the details of the past few weeks. In a very unexpected manner, the father indicated that he and his wife had a few questions about life after death. I nodded and encouraged them to ask away. While the questions were broad and general, it was clear that the parents were really asking about the whereabouts and status of their beloved deceased children.

The Spirit of the Lord came upon me in such a powerful

way that I had difficulty controlling my emotions. I don't recall all of what I said in the moments that followed, but I do remember speaking these words: "Your children died before the age of accountability and are therefore saved in the celestial kingdom of heaven. Their exaltation is secure. Their place with God and their opportunity for continuing growth and development and expansion are certain. The question is not what will become of them but rather what will become of you. Will you one day be with them? Will your family be intact? Will the two of you have the opportunity of raising them to maturity and resuming the sweet and tender family associations you once knew? The answers to those questions are less certain. It all depends on you—whether you decide to face life squarely, remember why you came to earth in the first place, remember the covenants you made in the holy temple, and place your complete trust and confidence in our Savior Jesus Christ." I then added: "You need to come back to church, to take the sacrament, to be a part of a ward family that will welcome you with open arms. I promise you if you will get back on course and pray with all your might for your burdens to be lifted, you will know, before too very long, the peace that passes all understanding."

After we had prayer, I turned to the husband and said, "I will pick you up on Sunday morning for priesthood meeting at 8:45 A.M." The brother recoiled and said, "Wait a minute. I'm not sure I'm ready for that yet." I came right back: "I'll see you at 8:45." I was there on Sunday morning, he was dressed, and we went to priesthood meeting together. His family joined him for Sunday School. And I think you could probably tell the rest of the story. Now I know that not every case of working with less-active members should be handled in this particular way (a most direct way, to be sure), but this one was, and it took. As home teachers, priesthood representatives of our God, we have a responsibility to do more than socialize with our families, though that is an important part of what we do. We are charged to "watch over the church always, and be with and strengthen them," to insure that "all the members do their duty." In short, we are to invite the children of God to come unto Christ (see D&C 20:53, 55, 59).

Every man who receives the Melchizedek Priesthood enters into a covenant with God, a covenant that requires that we as holders of the Priesthood magnify our callings (D&C 84:33). The Prophet Joseph Smith is reported to have explained that "to magnify a calling is to hold it up in dignity and importance, that the light of heaven may shine through one's performance to the gaze of other men. An elder magnifies his calling when he learns what his duties as an elder are and then performs them" (cited by Monson in Conference Report, April 2006, 59). We as covenant people thereby become a light to the world, a means by which men and women of every nation and clime are enabled to witness the power of the Almighty in their midst, a means by which people of other faiths become privy to the fruits of the work of the ministry.

President Gordon B. Hinckley has taught: "We are all in this great endeavor together. We are here to assist our Father in His work and His glory, 'to bring to pass the immortality and eternal life of man' (Moses 1:39). Your obligation is as serious in your sphere of responsibility as is my obligation in my sphere. No calling in this church is small or of little consequence. All of us in the pursuit of our duty touch the lives of others." President Hinckley also offered this marvelous promise: "You have as great an opportunity for satisfaction in the performance of your duty as I do in mine. The progress of this work will be determined by our joint efforts. Whatever your calling, it is as fraught with the same kind of opportunity to accomplish good as is mine. What is really important is that this is the work of the Master. Our work is to go about doing good, as did He" (Conference Report, April 1995, 94).

King Benjamin explained that we come to *know* those whom we serve (see Mosiah 5:13). In that sense, one of the greatest blessings that can come to us through serving our King is that we come to know him—not just to know about him, but to know him. In the process, we will come to love him in ways we cannot now fathom. "What we need," Elder Henry B. Eyring declared, "is faith in Him and to love Him. We must know that He lives and who He is. When we do, we will love Him. . . . As we plead for help in His service, the Holy Ghost will come and confirm our faith in Him. Our faith in the Savior will increase. And, as we continue to serve Him, we will come to love Him. *To be called to serve is a call to come to love the Master we serve. It is a call to have our natures changed"* (in Conference Report, April 2006, 16; emphasis added).

My father was able to face death without fear because he had, for many years, given heart and soul to serve his Heavenly King. People do not remember that he served as the first bishop of the Baker Ward as much as they remember that he was the life of the party and that he loved being among the people of God. People do not remember so much about his service in the stake presidency, but they remember that he preached the gospel with great power and persuasion, that he laid hands upon many who were sick or afflicted and healed them, and that he brought comfort and assurance and perspective through his funeral sermons. People do not remember much about how he conducted meetings or what kind of administrator he was, but his early-morning seminary students, now grandparents themselves, have glowing memories of what it was like to study the gospel and search the scriptures with him day by day. I don't remember how much money Dad made or exactly what positions he occupied in the business world, but I will always remember how he led us in family prayer, how he taught us in family home evening, how he insisted on being at church fifteen to twenty minutes early. Dad gave his heart and soul to the King, and I can picture him one day receiving the sweet certification and welcome: "Come unto me, ye blessed, there is a place prepared for you in the mansions of my Father" (Enos 1:27).

Dad was a priesthood man, a servant of the Heavenly King, and I want to go where he goes.

POINTS TO PONDER

1. What is it about death that impels me to focus on things of primary importance? Just how different is my typical perspective while I face each day as opposed to the day when death stares me in the face?

2. As I ponder the various overarching and undergirding messages of scripture, what things do I suppose will be of greatest concern to God on the day of judgment? What areas of my life will concern him the most?

3. How can I go about gaining an eye single to the glory of God (D&C 88:67)? It was the Danish philosopher Sören Kierkegaard who taught that "purity of heart is to will one thing." What did he mean?

4. If in fact the seriousness with which I take my home teaching assignment is a fairly accurate measure of how I view my own role within the work of the kingdom, what does my own record suggest? What must be done in order to gain the spirit of my calling and a witness of the significance of the duty of a home teacher?

ONE UNITED THRONG

WHILE THE STRENGTH of the Church of Jesus Christ derives largely from the solid core of individual witness and conversion, there is power, consummate power, in unity. There is power in numbers, power in people with "like precious faith" (2 Peter 1:1) who join together to lend their gifts and talents and energies in the supernal cause of our Savior and Redeemer.

I remember distinctly the feeling of personal loss and even a bit of fear as our family moved from the Baton Rouge area to a small community to the north called Baker. New neighbors. New friends. A new world. And, of course, a new branch of the Church. I recall asking Mom and Dad why we couldn't continue to attend our ward in Baton Rouge, one in which I had essentially grown up, one whose members I had come to trust and love. It was then that I learned for the first time that as Latter-day Saints we are counseled to attend church according to our geography, not our desires. We found ourselves within the boundaries of what was a brand-new branch of The Church of Jesus Christ of Latter-day Saints. Although I did recognize a few faces, most of the folks were total strangers.

What was really unsettling was that we were also asked to leave our beautiful little chapel on Hiawatha Street and hold our meetings elsewhere; in this case, we did not have a chapel. Instead, we attended church in the girl's gymnasium at the high school where I was beginning the ninth grade. In a gym! Because the community was largely Baptist, I was asked quite often through the next couple of years, "Where is your church located?" and I would answer timidly, embarrassed (and in quiet tones), "In the girl's gym." I don't remember anyone laughing out loud, but I did receive my share of strange looks. Our goal, as a small group of Saints, was to raise enough money to build our own chapel (back then, you recall, the local units were required to raise a significant portion of the overall building cost). The familiar "building fund" was forever before us; we must have had a hundred chicken dinners, spaghetti dinners, donut sales, softball tournaments (where members of our branch handled the concessions), car washes, and myriad other activities with one aim in mind—to build the first phase of a three-phase church building in Baker. At first it seemed a strange thing to be asked to do, but as time went by and as we began to rub shoulders with one another in the endeavor, it became both fun and fulfilling.

A tremendous amount of work went on during those

beginning years under the direction of Brother Burt Clark, the first branch president; and in the early 1960s the Baker Ward was organized and my father was called as the first bishop. I didn't understand the specifics of the fund-raising and exactly what our relationship with the general Church was (and still don't), but one event is burned into my memory and my soul. Not recalling the details, I simply remember Dad standing up before the body of priesthood holders and saying, essentially, "Brethren, we have a problem. We have a payment of fifteen hundred dollars due to the Church in just a few days. I don't know how else to meet that need quickly except to ask for your help. I know each of you has done all you can to pay into the building fund and that we have worked ourselves to death to raise the needed monies. But we're short. And I don't know what else to do except ask you to contribute more. If you're not able to help right now, I understand. Just do what you can." Dad then turned to one of the brethren on the first row and asked to borrow his hat. My father reached into his back pocket, pulled out his wallet, took out all the cash he had, put it into the hat, and handed the hat to the first man on the first row. It was a simple gesture but, for my father, a terribly difficult thing to do. I then saw the miracle unfold as each man and boy, one by one, put bills or coins or a check into the hat. Dad then took the time to count the money and, through his tears, thank these "mighty men of valor" for giving all they had. It was enough and to spare.

I loved those marvelous men before the passing of the hat, but it is difficult to describe what I felt when that session was completed. Now, almost fifty years later, there burns in my soul a firm conviction that there is power in unity, sweet power in toiling together in the work of the Almighty, dynamic power associated with acting as a group in the name of the Lord. And, of course, after we had raised the funds, we began work on the chapel (you may remember that local members were then allowed to contribute significantly to the construction itself, which we did almost every day), a work that has left me with scars (from sliding down the roof), deformed toenails (from heavy weights being dropped on my feet), and a weak back (from lifting much more weight than I should have at that young age). But it has also left me changed in more poignant ways: there is an indelible seal of satisfaction in my soul, a quiet but overwhelming sense of accomplishment, and, above all, a penetrating love for my brethren of the priesthood and especially for that God whose servants they are. I am not the same now because of the united power of the priesthood I witnessed and contributed to then.

A few years ago while visiting my mother, I drove out to the Baker Ward with my youngest son. I reminisced about how that beautiful property had once been nothing but swampland and how a few weak and simple people, led and empowered by the priesthood of God, had, in a Southern setting "made the desert to blossom as a rose." As I went on and on to Stephen about what that building represented (and, bless his heart, he was trying to be courteous and attentive), I realized that there was something of me in that edifice, that whatever puny sacrifice I had made in time and energy had been transformed into commitment and conviction and dedication to the work of the kingdom of God. Those who invest themselves in a righteous cause come to be filled with love and loyalty to that cause.

Who can measure the power of godliness that lies within our grasp, to some extent largely untapped? Who can fathom what would happen if we men of the priesthood recognized what we have, denied ourselves of ungodliness and worldly lusts, put away trivialities and telestial distractions, and devoted ourselves earnestly as one united throng to the tasks at hand? It would be as though God had spoken the immortal words to us (instead of Moses and the children of Israel): "Fear ye not, stand still, and see the salvation of the Lord" (Exodus 14:13). Or, as Joseph Smith recorded in Liberty Jail: "Therefore, dearly beloved brethren, let us cheerfully do all things that lie in our power; and then may we stand still, with the utmost assurance, to see the salvation of God, and for his arm to be revealed" (D&C 123:17).

One of the almost undiscovered spiritual resources in our midst is the priesthood quorum. Many years ago President Stephen L Richards taught that every priesthood quorum is intended to serve three main functions: (1) a class, (2) a service agency, and (3) a brotherhood (in Conference Report,

October 1938, 117). First, we are a *class,* a place where the doctrines of the kingdom are taught, where we are instructed concerning the covenants and ordinances (see D&C 107:89), where we learn our duties and are built up in the faith. "An elders quorum should be a school of the prophets," Elder Bruce R. McConkie pointed out, "a place where every elder and prospective elder learns what he and his family must do to gain peace in this life and eternal life in the world to come" ("Only an Elder," 68).

Second, we are a *service agency.* Not only should we respond to the call to participate in work projects (to the extent that we are physically able), but we are also to search out opportunities to express love and extend service to the members of the household of faith. More than once I have witnessed a group of men within a priesthood quorum or group recognize a pressing need of a member of the quorum, talk among themselves, and act quickly to resolve the problem. They didn't wait to be assigned; they acted.

A priesthood quorum is and should be a *brotherhood.* In fact, the most important organization to which any man belongs, other than his own family, is his quorum or group. Note the following statements from our leaders:

Joseph F. Smith: "We expect to see the day, if we live long enough (and if some of us do not live long enough to see it, there are others who will), when every council of the Priesthood in The Church of Jesus Christ of Latter-day Saints will understand its duty; will assume its own responsibility, will magnify its calling, and fill its place in the Church to the uttermost, according to the intelligence and ability possessed by it. When that day shall come, there will not be so much necessity for work that is now being done by the auxiliary organizations, because it will be done by the regular quorums of the Priesthood. The Lord designed and comprehended it from the beginning, and he has made provision in the Church whereby every need may be met and satisfied through the regular organizations of the Priesthood. It has truly been said that the Church is perfectly organized. The only trouble is that these organizations are not fully alive to the obligations that rest upon them. When they become thoroughly awakened to the requirements made of them, they will fulfil their duties more faithfully, and the work of the Lord will be all the stronger and more powerful and influential in the world" (*Gospel Doctrine*, 159–60).

J. Reuben Clark Jr.: "The priesthood quorums in their extending of relief do not have the obligation prescribed to the bishop. But the relationships of the priesthood, [and] the spirit of lofty unselfish brotherhood which it carries with it, do require that they individually and as quorums exert their utmost means and powers to rehabilitate, spiritually and temporally, their erring and their unfortunate brethren" ("Spiritual and Temporal Rehabilitation," 731).

Harold B. Lee: "All Priesthood quorums are 'commanded' [by the Lord] to marshal their forces and, under the spirit and power of the Priesthood, to see to it that every person who is in distress is assisted by his quorum to become self-sustaining" ("The Place of the Priesthood Quorum," 634).

Gordon B. Hinckley: "I am satisfied, my brethren, that there is enough of expertise, of knowledge, of strength, of concern in every priesthood quorum to assist the troubled members of that quorum if these resources are properly administered" (*Teachings of Gordon B. Hinckley,* 489).

Gordon B. Hinckley: "It will be a marvelous day, my brethren—it will be a day of fulfillment of the purposes of the Lord—when our priesthood quorums become an anchor of strength to every man belonging thereto, when each such man may appropriately be able to say, 'I am a member of a priesthood quorum of The Church of Jesus Christ of Latter-day Saints. I stand ready to assist my brethren in all of their needs, as I am confident they stand ready to assist me in mine. Working together, we shall grow spiritually as covenant sons of God. Working together, we can stand, without embarrassment and without fear, against every wind of adversity that might blow, be it economic, social, or spiritual'" (*Teachings of Gordon B. Hinckley,* 490).

In addition to participating in and building our quorums, we need to reach out to those not of our faith. Elder Orson F. Whitney observed that "God is using more than one people for the accomplishment of his great and marvelous work. The Latter-day Saints cannot do it all. It is too vast, too arduous, for any one people" (in Conference Report, April 1928, 59). While on the one hand the Saints of the Most

High are to eschew all forms of evil and reject each and every effort to dilute the divine or corrupt the truth, yet we are commissioned to be a leavening influence among the people of the earth. We cannot make our influence felt if we completely avoid the troublesome issues in society and insulate ourselves and our families from today's challenges.

As members of the Church of Jesus Christ, we have a responsibility to love and care for our neighbors and make a difference for good in their lives. Perhaps they will join our Church, but perhaps they will not. Whether they do or not, we have been charged by our Lord and Master, as well as his chosen spokesmen, to love them, to serve them, and to treat them with the same respect and kindness that we would extend to a person of our own faith.

There is a very real sense in which the Latter-day Saints are a part of the larger "body of Christ," the Christian community. Given the challenges we face in our society—fatherless homes, child and spouse abuse, divorce, poverty, spreading crime and delinquency, spiritual wickedness in high places—it seems so foolish for men and women who claim to believe in the Lord and Savior, whose hearts and lives have been surrendered to that Savior, to allow doctrinal differences to prevent them from working together. Do we agree on the problems in our world? Do we agree on the fact that most all of these ills have moral or spiritual roots?

President Gordon B. Hinckley pleaded with us: "We can respect other religions and must do so. We must recognize the great good they accomplish. We must teach our children to be tolerant and friendly toward those not of our faith. We can and do work with those of other religions in the defense of those values which have made our civilization great and our society distinctive" (in Conference Report, April 1998, 3).

My recent interactions with men and women of various faiths have had a profound impact on me; they have broadened my horizons dramatically and reminded me—a sobering reminder we all need once in a while—that we are all sons and daughters of the same Eternal Father. We may never resolve our differences on the Godhead or the Trinity, on the spiritual or corporeal nature of Deity, or on the sufficiency of the Bible, but we can agree that salvation is in Christ; that the ultimate transformation of society will come only through the application of Christian solutions to pressing moral issues; and that the regeneration of individual hearts and souls is foundational to the restoration of virtue in our communities and nations.

The older I get, the less prone I am to believe in coincidence. Like you, I believe that God has a divine plan—not only a plan for the ultimate establishment of the kingdom of God on earth, but also an individualized plan for you and me. I gladly and eagerly acknowledge his hand in all things, including the orchestration of events in our lives and the interlacing of our daily associations. I believe he brings people into our path who can bless and enlighten us, and I know that he brings us into contact with people whose acquaintanceship will, down the road, open doors, dissolve barriers, and make strait the way of the Lord. The prayer of Elisha for the young lad seems particularly pertinent to our work: "Lord, I pray thee, open [our] eyes, that [we] may see" (2 Kings 6:17).

Much is said in our expanding world about the need to celebrate diversity. Of course we are a diverse community; that is how a society like ours is constituted. But our strength is not to be found in our diversity; our power to influence the world for good will not come through our diversity. Some seem to act as though the Lord has said, "Be diverse, and if ye are not diverse, ye are not mine." No, we are to strive to achieve unity in spite of our diversity. "We are seeking to establish a oneness," Elder John Taylor observed, "under the guidance and direction of the Almighty. . . . If there is any principle for which we contend with greater tenacity than another, it is this oneness. . . . *To the world this principle is a gross error, for amongst them it is every man for himself; every man follows his own ideas, his own religion, his own morals, and the course in everything that suits his own notions. But the Lord dictates differently. We are under His guidance, and we should seek to be one with him and with all the authorities of His Church and kingdom on the earth in all the affairs of life. . . .* This is what we are after, and when we have attained to this ourselves, we want to teach the nations of the earth the same pure principles that have emanated from the Great Eloheim. We want Zion to rise and shine that the glory of God may be manifest in her midst. . . . We never intend to stop until this point is attained through the teaching and guidance of the Lord and our obedience to His laws. Then, *when men say unto us, 'you are not like us,' we reply, 'we know it; we do not want to be. We want to be like the Lord, we want to secure His favor and approbation and to live under His smile, and to acknowledge, as ancient Israel did on a certain occasion, 'The Lord is our God, our judge, and our king, and He shall reign over us.''* (*Journal of Discourses*, 11:346–47; emphasis added).

In short, the more we can broaden our brotherhood and sisterhood, extending it beyond those of our own faith to include noble men and women of other faiths, the better. That "one united throng" thereby becomes a powerful and even unstoppable influence for good, a light that will shine brilliantly in a darkened world, the sound of a trumpet that is sure and certain (1 Corinthians 14:8) in a warring world of competing and corrupt voices and values.

Finally, I'd like to share an experience that is not terribly unusual, but one that taught me at the time the value of working together as men and women of faith, as well as the power of priesthood. During one of the times I was serving as bishop, one of our valued and beloved high priests came to me and confided that he had been diagnosed with cancer, and that the prognosis was not good. We wept together as we discussed his situation, his concerns for wife and family, and how best to prepare for what lay ahead. I asked him if he would mind if his secret were shared with the members of the ward. He commented that he really didn't want to burden

others or have people too focused upon him and his problems. I then opened the Book of Mormon and read to him
verses that he knew very well—that it is our responsibility and
our privilege as covenant followers of the Christ to bear one
another's burdens, to mourn with those who mourn (Mosiah
18:8–9), to both metaphorically and literally put our arms
around one another and face difficulties and trials together.
He nodded and submitted to my request. I suggested that we
set a date to fast together as a ward and then to retire to the
bishop's office for a priesthood blessing. He agreed hesitantly
but gratefully.

I remember announcing our brother's situation to the
ward in sacrament meeting, testifying of the power of fasting
and prayer, and calling upon the ward to fast and importune
the Lord with all their souls for a special blessing in behalf of
our dear friend. We did so. We began our fast together the
next Saturday and closed our fast as a group in a short meeting after sacrament meeting. We sang hymns and prayed. I
spoke briefly on what a wonderful thing it was that we could
come together as a body of believers, as followers of the Great
Physician, and petition the heavens for divine intervention. I
called upon one of our great old high priests, a man of
tremendous steadiness and spirituality, to offer the benedic-
tion to our gathering. It was a prayer that was given from
above, one of those rare moments when we were able to lay
our united burden upon the altar and confidently let God

take over. Following the prayer many of us remained in our seats and rejoiced in the spirit of what we felt together.

After the congregation had embraced and expressed their love and support for our beloved friend, they all filed quietly out of the chapel. My counselors and I then made our way into the bishop's office and exercised the priesthood in behalf of one whose association we cherished and whose company we simply were not ready to surrender to death. Again, the Spirit of God was poured out upon us, the powers of the priesthood were manifest richly, and words were spoken as from the midst of eternity. Our friend was told that his time for graduation was not yet, that the Almighty had more things for him to accomplish in his family and in the Church. He was needed on earth. Indeed, within a matter of days I felt impressed to call him as the Young Men's president, which, of course, is a very demanding calling, in terms of both time and energy. He performed magnificently, just as I (and the Lord) knew he would. He lived several more years and blessed a multitude of people.

I often praise God for the opportunity to have been involved in such a sweet labor, a labor of love that reminds us that no man or woman is an island and that there is consummate power in unity and supernal power in the priesthood. It is a power just waiting to be tapped.

POINTS TO PONDER

1. The Savior has taught us in a modern revelation that if we are not united we are not His (D&C 38:27). To what extent am I striving for unity of soul, that is, unity within my own heart and mind? To what extent am I striving for unity within my home and in my associations outside the home? What are some barriers to unity?

2. Just how close do I feel to the members of my priesthood quorum? What can I do to become a stronger contributor to the unity and brotherhood of the quorum?

3. What is my relationship with persons of other faiths? What have I done lately to build greater understanding and disabuse them of misunderstanding? What would happen if I prayed for God to help me to see those of other faiths as he sees them and to feel for them what he feels?

4. How has my service as a priesthood holder affected the larger society? What are some ways that I can influence a world filled with eroding moral values through standing up and proclaiming the principles of the restored gospel of Jesus Christ?

TREADING WHERE HIS
FEET HAVE TROD

IN BEING ORDAINED to the holy priesthood, we receive a divine investiture of authority: we are called and charged to speak and act as our Lord would do. More specifically, we are called upon to exercise our agency properly. There is a very real sense in which followers of the Christ do not have the right to do wrong. God is our Principal, and we are his agents. Our agency is thus defined as our commission to carry out his will in the way he wants it carried out. Or, as one verse in the Doctrine and Covenants states, "Wherefore, as ye are agents, ye are on the Lord's errand; and whatsoever ye do according to the will of the Lord is the Lord's business" (D&C 64:29). "The *capacity* to do evil and the *right* to do evil are very different things," Joseph Fielding McConkie pointed out. "No one has ever done anything that was wrong with the approbation of heaven" (*Understanding the Power God Gives Us,* 11; emphasis added). A Book of Mormon prophet taught that "the Messiah cometh in the fulness of time, that he may redeem the children of men from the fall. And because that they are redeemed from the fall they have become free forever, knowing good from evil; to act for themselves and not to be acted upon" (2 Nephi 2:26). This passage "is telling us that because of the atonement of Christ, we are free to act for ourselves. [It] does not suggest, however, that the Atonement gives us any 'right' to do evil" (McConkie, *Understanding the Power God Gives Us,* 12).

With these truths in mind, President Joseph Fielding Smith was bold in declaring: "I have heard people say, and members of the Church too, 'I have a right to do as I please.' My answer is: No, you do not. You haven't any right at all to do just as you please. There is only one right that you have, and that is to . . . keep the commandments of Jesus Christ. He has a perfect right to tell us so. We have no right to refuse. I do not care who the man is; I do not care where he lives, or what he is—when the gospel of Jesus Christ is presented to him, he has no right to refuse to receive it. He has the privilege. He is not compelled to receive it, because our Father in heaven has given to every one of us, in the Church and out, the gift of . . . agency. That . . . agency gives us the privilege to accept and be loyal to our Lord's commandments, but it has never given us the right to reject them. Every man who rejects the commandments of our Father in heaven is rebellious" (Conference Report, April 1967, 120–21).

Freedom comes to the soul of one who has surrendered

unconditionally to God, who has chosen to do things God's way. That is, "No man is like God unless he is free. God is free. Why? Because He possesses all righteousness, all power, and all wisdom. He also possesses His agency, and His agency is exercised in doing that which is good, and not that which is evil. So no man can be like unto Him until he can subject himself unto that which is righteous, pure, and good, and until he can forsake error and sin and overcome himself" (*Teachings of the Presidents of the Church—Joseph F. Smith,* 292).

If we are to tread where the King of kings trod, we must search the scriptures, search the revelations, study his person and his personality, and seek the Spirit. We must pay particular attention to how Jesus treated people, for therein is one of the keys to understanding his magnificence and his greatness. To put this another way, there was something highly unusual about Jesus, something beautiful about the way people were drawn to him, especially those who were considered to be on the outskirts of social acceptance in the first century: tax collectors, shepherds, fishermen, and even prostitutes. They felt warm and welcome when in his presence, in spite of the fact that many of them lived in violation of social standards or even Mosaic law. The power of his love was of such magnitude that they did not feel condemned or judged by him, and we are left to ask ourselves the haunting question: Why is it, on too many occasions, that these same kinds of people do not feel comfortable in our presence today? Perhaps we have unwittingly created in the Christian church a climate and an atmosphere of respectability that makes the smoker, the drinker, the poor, and the long-time wanderer feel less than welcome about joining us. Jesus was absolutely unaffected by this world's pecking order and cared precious little for earthly applause or mortal medals. He did care—indeed, he cared deeply—about people's hearts, about what they longed for, about what they hurt over, about how they felt. Jesus' worldview was expansive enough to include any and all who chose to come unto him. Every man and woman who humbled themselves, confessed their weakness, and acknowledged their need for his saving help always felt comfortable and at ease in his presence.

Jesus was downright revolutionary in the way he treated women in his day. To put it bluntly, women of the first century had little say, were seldom if ever listened to, and had few rights. Everyone understood that a woman's word could never be relied upon in a court of law. But along came Jesus, and he changed everything. He taught women, he talked to women, he ministered to women, and he was open to their adoration and worship. There is a model here for every man who has been called to bear the holy priesthood: we will know a great deal about a man's soul and about his standing before God when we know how he feels toward and treats women, especially those nearest and dearest to him. I have often been sobered by the thought that my own two daughters' impressions of what their Heavenly Father is like have been developed, in a measure at least, through how they viewed me. Further, I feel immensely grateful for the way my father treated my mother; he was not only respectful and deferential to her—always making it clear to us that, other than God, she was his highest priority—but they had an equal partnership in every phase of life. Dad would never have considered making a major decision without first discussing it with Mom and would have moved forward only when there was consensus between them.

While I think my wife would be the first to acknowledge that I have not been a perfect husband or father, I have tried to make it very clear to my children and grandchildren that the most important mortal relationship in my life is my relationship with Shauna. It has always seemed clear that for me to make major decisions regarding purchases or moves or employment without discussing it with my sweetheart is in fact an act of unrighteous dominion and something about which the Lord has given stern warning (D&C 121:34–40; Hunter, Conference Report, October 1994, 68–69). The sobering fact is that I cannot expect to enjoy the love of, the blessings of, and a closeness to the King of kings unless I am helping to create an atmosphere of love and trust and intimacy and respect within my own home. Power in the priesthood comes to those who utilize that priesthood worthily and who act within the bounds the Lord has set—by "persuasion, by long-suffering, by gentleness and meekness, and by love unfeigned; by kindness, and pure knowledge, which shall greatly enlarge the soul without hypocrisy and without guile" (D&C 121:41–42).

To tread where our Lord's feet have trod is to learn by experience, but more especially through spiritual and moral transformation, how not to take offense. It has been my blessing as a priesthood leader to have met with many young engaged couples seeking a final piece of advice. What is interesting to me is that when I first started offering advice in the late 1970s I would spend a hour or two with the couple, making known to them my sacred list of sixty-four things that must be done in order for them to have a successful marriage. As the years passed, however, the items on the list decreased in number and my counsel became much, much simpler. Most recently, I sat with my own daughter and her fiancé and offered only two pieces of advice, which are actually two sides of the same coin. I promised them that if they would apply this principle early in their marriage and hold tenaciously to it, they would enjoy a rich and rewarding union, one that would bring heaven down to earth. The two pieces of counsel were simply (1) choose not to take offense, and (2) assume the best. There is so much bickering and badgering, suspicion and paranoia, silence and indifference, ugliness and pain in marriages today, and most all of it is so very unnecessary.

Suppose I come home from work late one afternoon and find my wife very quiet and reserved. I ask how her day has gone and she snaps back, "Oh great. Just great! Any other questions?" (I'd better add a disclaimer at this point that this story is completely hypothetical!) What's my response? The natural man in me is prone to think: "Well, if that's the way she's going to be, I'll stay out of her way. You would think she'd be a little more appreciative for how hard I work. You'd think she could treat me with a tiny bit of respect. I'll show her—I'll go into the silent treatment." Not an atypical response, I would suppose. But not a very helpful one either. How should a Priesthood Man respond?

Let's just ask ourselves: Does Shauna love me? Of course she does; I know that. Do you suppose her intention is to hurt me, to belittle me, to make me feel unwanted and unloved? I wouldn't think so. Clearly something has happened today that has upset her, set her on edge, or perhaps even frightened her. Is it possible for me to assume the best about my wife's mood, assume that there's obviously something going on within her that is painful? I don't know what it is yet, but until I do, I can make the effort to provide a patient and loving environment. I might ask her, gently: "Sweetheart, is there anything you'd like to talk about? Clearly something is troubling you." She may say: "No, I don't want to talk about it," at which point I back off and honor her hesitation to talk. I help out around the house the best I can and allow her the space and acceptance she needs for now. I think that's how Jesus would handle things; I think that's how he would want his priesthood representatives to respond as well.

Choosing not to take offense and assuming the best have

not been easy attitudes and approaches for me to acquire, but I've worked at it and pleaded with the Lord for his help for many years now. I have not arrived, but I feel like I'm getting there gradually, if the Savior and those closest to me will allow me a little more time. A typical reaction to such a scene now would be for me to go into the bedroom, hang up my coat and tie, sit on the edge of the bed, and ask myself: "Am I going to take offense or not?" More and more often I find myself saying, "No, I am going to assume the best, and I am going to respond with love." Now that's real progress for me, but I long for the day to come when I don't even have to think about it, where no decision is required at all, where my mind and heart have been so transformed by the power of the Spirit (see Romans 12:1–2) that I spontaneously feel and act lovingly.

Larry Crabb, a respected Christian counselor, has written: "One friend comes to mind who is self-disciplined in his health habits. He resists the temptation to eat too many sweets, he jogs faithfully, and he paces his workload well. I respect him for that. His behavior reflects a commendable level of willpower, a level that sometimes puts to shame my efforts to eat, exercise, and work properly.

"Another friend responds to a terribly disappointing and painful struggle in his life by loving others more deeply. He feels his pain but somehow uses it to make himself more aware of others' pain and of God's ability to encourage. When

I look at his life, words like noble, godly, and rich come to mind.

"Observing habits of self-discipline, orderliness, and general cordiality do not bring to mind those same words. I describe my well-disciplined friend as effective, respectable, and nice. When I look at his life I think, 'I should be more disciplined,' I feel a bit pressured, somewhat guilty, and occasionally motivated. The effect of my struggling friend, on the other hand, is not to make me say, 'I should be more disciplined,' but 'I want to be more loving.'

"The difference is enormous. Some people push me to do better by trying harder. Others draw me to be better by enticing me with an indefinable quality about their lives that seems to grow out of an unusual relationship with Christ, one that really means something, one that goes beyond correct doctrine and appropriate dedication to personally felt reality. . . .

"I want to do more than exercise kindness toward my wife; I want to freely give to her from deep resources within me. I want to do more than teach my kids what's expected and then enforce rules to keep them in line; I want to draw them by my life into the pursuit of God. I want to do more than preach sermons that are [scripturally] sound, well delivered, and warmly received; I want to pour out my soul in ways that convey truth with personal power. I want to do more than control my tendency toward depression; I want to taste the goodness of God" (*Inside Out*, 41–42).

In short, the Lord seeks to transform our nature, not just to modify our behavior. The gospel of Jesus Christ is the power by which we learn to root out the causes of our spiritual illness rather than devoting all our time and exhausting our strength in the alleviation of symptoms.

While most all of us have miles and miles to go before we rest (in terms of our spiritual maturity and thus our capacity to forgive in this manner), our Lord holds out the ideal: he models the fact that you and I can find greater joy and fulfillment, can see greater purpose in life, and can avoid the unnecessary burdens of grudges and unconfronted memories by choosing not to take offense. As John MacArthur has written, "If anyone ever had good reason not to forgive, it was the Lord Jesus. He was the ultimate and only true victim—totally innocent of any wrongdoing. He never wronged another individual, never spoke a lie, never committed an unkind or unloving act, never broke the law of God, never had an impure thought. He never yielded to any evil temptation whatsoever. . . .

"No one was *less* worthy of death than He. Even the evil Roman governor Pontius Pilate testified repeatedly, 'I find no guilt in this man.' . . .

"Forgiveness was what filled his heart, not condemnation or revenge" (*Freedom and Power of Forgiveness,* 31, 32).

As we mentioned earlier, Jesus ate and drank with sinners. He occasionally companied with those who were considered to be on the lower crust of society. He befriended the underdog and was kind to the castoff. Because there was no insecurity within him, because he was always guided by the knowledge of who he was and Whose he was, he felt no need to put on airs, manage appearances, or be socially selective. When someone spoke to Jesus, surely they had his full attention.

It is too easy for those of us who aspire to Christian discipleship to be driven by what others think, to allow our conversation and our conduct to be determined by less than noble motives. It is too simple to be drawn into duplicity, to become obsessed with whose opinion matters and whose company would bring the most acclaim. But the lowly Nazarene calls his priesthood bearers to a higher righteousness. He bids us to follow where he has led, to become a friend to all. I know what it feels like to be conversing with someone only to have that conversation interrupted by a man or woman of greater social stature. I know what it feels like for the person with whom I was conversing to then ignore or shun me, to turn his attention to the one who seems to matter most at the moment. I also have been in the presence of persons whose hearts are unconcerned with society's pecking order, men and women who love people, not position. The former category of persons are those who tend to distinguish people in terms of rank and place in society; theirs is a degrading and demoralizing perspective and influence. On the other hand, those who have risen above the temptation to exclude or divide or distinguish in terms of getting ahead make a significant difference in the world. They bless lives.

In a modern revelation the Lord sets forth a fact that we all understand: Joseph Smith, while a prophet of God and the Lord's appointed spokesman, was not perfect. "There are those who have sought occasion against him without cause; nevertheless, he has sinned; but verily I say unto you, I, the Lord, forgive sins unto those who confess their sins before me and ask forgiveness, who have not sinned unto death." We are then given insight into a deeply significant point: that it is one thing to express forgiveness with the mouth, to say that all is well, to profess that you have moved on—and quite another to forgive our offender *in our hearts.* "My disciples, in days of old, sought occasion against one another and forgave not one another in their hearts; and for this evil they were afflicted and sorely chastened" (D&C 64:6–8).

"So many of us are prone to say we forgive," President Gordon B. Hinckley pointed out, "when in fact we are unwilling to forget. If the Lord is willing to forget the sins of the repentant, then why are so many of us inclined to bring up the past again and again? Here is a great lesson we all need to learn. There is no true forgiveness without forgetting" (*Teachings of Gordon B. Hinckley,* 230).

I am very much aware that there are those who have been subjected to much pain and distress in their lives, to abuse, to neglect, to the agonies of wanting more than anything to live a normal life and to feel normal feelings, but seem unable to do so. I would say, first of all, that each of us, whoever we are, wrestles with something. Perhaps it's stuff that passes in time like a phase. Perhaps it's the torture of watching helplessly as loved ones choose unwisely and thereby close doors of opportunity for themselves and foreclose future privileges. And then there are the terrible traumas in our lives, those occasions when someone we love does injury to our tender trust and deals a blow that strikes at the center of all we hold dear and all we value about ourselves.

I know that the day is coming when all the wrongs, the awful wrongs of this life, will be righted. I bear witness that the God of justice will attend to all evil. And I certify that those things that are beyond our power to control will be corrected, either here or hereafter. Many of us may come to enjoy the lifting, liberating powers of the Atonement in this life, and in such cases all our losses will be made up before we pass from this sphere of existence. Perhaps others of us will wrestle all our days with our traumas, for He who orchestrates the events of our lives will surely fix the time of our release. I have a conviction that when a person passes through the veil of death, all those impediments and challenges and crosses that were beyond his or her power to control—abuse, neglect, immoral environment, weighty traditions, and so forth—will be torn away like a film, and perfect peace will prevail in our hearts. "Some frustrations," Elder Boyd K. Packer taught, "we must endure without really solving the problem. Some things that ought to be put in order are not put in order because we cannot control them. Things we cannot solve, we must survive" (Conference Report, October 1987, 20).

There is one final aspect of the Savior's life we might mention here, one with which those who represent him become well acquainted during our stay on this earth—namely, that he was required to walk alone for a season, to lose the sustaining spiritual influence of the Father during the agonizing hours in Gethsemane and on Golgotha. In the Garden, as the King of kings knelt as our royal substitute before the Father and thus became "sin for us" (2 Corinthians 5:21), he cried out from a depth of anguish no mortal can begin to comprehend: "O my Father, if it be possible, let this cup [the bitter cup, the symbol of the wrath of God] pass from me: nevertheless not as I will, but as thou wilt" (Matthew 26:39). While hanging on the accursed cross of Calvary, subject not only to the shame and ignominy and torturous pain of crucifixion but also subject once again to the loss of the Father's Spirit (see Young, *Journal of Discourses,* 3:205–6; Talmage, *Jesus the Christ,* 661; McConkie, Conference Report, April 1985, 10; *The Mortal Messiah,* 4:224–28), his soul cry was the prophetic fulfillment of the psalmic words, "My God, my God, why hast thou forsaken me?" (Matthew 27:46; Psalm 22:1).

Having entered in at the gate and received the covenant gospel, we claim the right to enjoy the constant companionship of the Holy Ghost, the right to enjoy the sweet comfort and direction and cleansing brought by the third member of the Godhead. But as Jesus taught Nicodemus, "The wind [Spirit] bloweth where it listeth [chooses], and thou hearest the sound [voice] thereof, but canst not tell whence it cometh, and whither it goeth; so is every one that is born of the Spirit" (John 3:8). That is to say, the Spirit is not something that may be controlled or confined or elicited or manufactured by man. The spirit of inspiration we feel today may not be what we feel tomorrow, even though we have done nothing to offend that sacred influence. The spirit of testimony we feel and enjoy today may or may not be exactly what we experience next week or next year. How often do some of us go to bed on a Sunday evening, alive and almost on fire with the power of the Spirit enjoyed that day, only to awaken several hours later to feel alone or empty or even deserted?

Elder Orson Pratt once commented that one of his greatest desires was to so live that he could be divinely directed in all the affairs of his life, such that "the path in which I should walk will be plain, the Spirit of God being as it were a lamp to my feet." He then went on to say: "Supposing a person were thus guided all the time, from waking in the morning until they retired to rest at night; . . . and this should be the uninterrupted condition of an individual, I ask, where would be his trials? This would lead us to ask, *Is it not absolutely necessary that God should in some measure, withhold even from those who walk before him in purity and integrity, a portion of his Spirit,* that they may prove to themselves, their families and neighbors, and to the heavens whether they are full of integrity even in times when they have not so much of the Spirit to guide and influence them? I think that this is really necessary, consequently I do not know that we have any reason to complain of the darkness which occasionally hovers over the mind" (*Journal of Discourses,* 15:233; emphasis added).

I have often reflected on the question: How would I act if it were possible to become invisible to all other mortals? What would I do differently if in fact God himself were not permitted to know my mind and observe my actions? What kind of a priesthood holder would I be if my deeds were known only to myself? It seems that God wants occasionally to see what we are made of, how determined we are to follow him and his laws, how committed and trusting we are of the Savior and his covenant promises—even when we do not enjoy an overwhelming outpouring of the Spirit to motivate and empower us. President Brigham Young thus replied that a man is sometimes left to his own resources to "act as an independent being . . . to see what he will do . . . and try his independency—*to be righteous in the dark*" (Cited by Faust, Conference Report, October 2005, 21; emphasis added).

Jesus Christ is the Holy One of Israel, and we as his agents are expected to be a holy people, a royal priesthood (1 Peter 2:9; see also Leviticus 11:44; 1 Peter 1:15–16). Jesus judged righteous judgment, and we are called upon to do the same (JST Matthew 7:1–2; John 7:24; 3 Nephi 27:27). Christ our Lord was more than willing to be inconvenienced, literally unable to withhold compassion from the troubled (JST Mark 7:22–23), and so must we become. Our Master Teacher defied the social strata of his day and associated with men and women of all stripes (Luke 15:1–2), and our capacity to look upon the heart rather than the outward appearance alone (1 Samuel 15:22; 16:7) should mirror his. The great "Apostle and High Priest of our profession" (Hebrews 3:1), our Priesthood Prototype, "went about doing good" (Acts 10:38). Such also is our charge, our duty, our eternal blessing.

POINTS TO PONDER

1. In reflecting on the life and ministry of our Lord Jesus Christ, how did the great "High Priest of our profession" (Hebrews 3:1) exercise his priesthood and bless the world around him?

2. The scriptures teach us that because of the Atonement of Christ we are agents unto ourselves, possessing the power to choose right from wrong, good from evil (2 Nephi 2:26). If God is my Principal, what kind of an agent am I (D&C 64:29)? How can I exercise my agency even more effectively?

3. Jesus treated women with a deference and a dignity that befitted divine womanhood. What do my daughters or my wife understand about the power and blessings of the priesthood as a result of their interactions with me? To what extent do I demonstrate respect, admiration, and sincere interest in the views of women within my circle of influence?

4. What must I do to reach the point where I no longer choose to take offense? In reflecting on the past week or month, what situations might have gone differently if I had assumed the best and chosen not to be offended?

6

A ROYAL PRIESTHOOD

THE BLESSINGS OF THE PRIESTHOOD come to us through the faithful exercise of that priesthood. In other words, men who desire to enjoy the fruits of God's power must learn to act by faith. There are few things as desperately needed in our day as is faith—faith in the unseen, or as one astute observer of Christianity has noted, "faith that bridges the chasm between what our minds can know and what our souls aspire after" (Muggeridge, *Jesus: The Man Who Lives*, 20).

Faith is not whimpering acquiescence, not timid and spineless hope for happiness and for pie in the sky in the great by and by. Faith is active. Faith is powerful. Faith is based on evidence, internal evidence, the kind of evidence acquired by men and women who search and pray and open themselves to the Infinite, who refuse to yield to cynicism or arrogance. We cannot enjoy power in the priesthood until we learn to act by faith.

Though one need not be simpleminded to have faith, one may need to be simple in his or her approach to life and its challenges in order to enjoy the fruits of faith. How open are we today to simple belief? Just how believing are we? How would we respond to the miraculous of days gone by? Malcolm Muggeridge has written: "In humanistic times like ours, a contemporary virgin—assuming there are any such— would regard a message from the Angel Gabriel that she might expect to give birth to a son to be called the Son of the Highest as ill-tidings of great sorrow and a slur on the local family-planning centre. It is, in point of fact, extremely improbable, under existing conditions, that Jesus would have been permitted to be born at all. Mary's pregnancy, in poor circumstances, and with the father unknown, would have been an obvious case for abortion; and her talk of having conceived as a result of the intervention of the Holy Ghost would have pointed to the need for psychiatric treatment, and made the case for terminating her pregnancy even stronger. Thus our generation, needing a Saviour more, per- haps, than any that has ever existed, would be too humane to allow one to be born; too enlightened to permit the Light of the World to shine in a darkness that grows ever more oppressive" (*Jesus: The Man Who Lives*, 19–20).

Sometimes faith requires us to act in the face of (what the world would consider to be) the absurd. Abraham was asked to put to death his beloved and long-awaited son Isaac, the one hope Abraham had of fulfilling the promise that his pos- terity would be as numberless as the sands upon the seashore or the stars in the heavens. Jehovah had spoken. Abraham had entered the realm of divine experience, knew the voice of the Lord, and knew that what he had encountered was real. Therefore, when the awful assignment came to offer up Isaac in sacrifice, he obeyed, even though, rationally speaking, there was no way the promises could thereafter be realized. But the Father of the Faithful had implicit trust in his God, "accounting that God was able to raise [Isaac] up, even from the dead" (Hebrews 11:19). Abraham knew God and he knew his purposes; the finite mind yielded to the Infinite, knowing fully that "whatever God requires is right, no matter what it is, although we may not see the reason thereof till long after the events transpire" (*Teachings of the Prophet Joseph Smith*, 256). His leap of faith was prerequisite to his ascent to glory. God knew all about Abraham, but in this case Abraham needed to know something about Abraham.

I am shocked and often surprised by the ways some of us often use the word *faith*. I hear a missionary in Vienna say: "Come on, Elder, where's your faith? Why, if we had the faith we could baptize this whole city!" I watch with some sorrow as well-meaning but insensitive souls explain to a grieving mother and father that if the family had sufficient faith, their fifteen-year-old daughter, who has struggled with multiple sclerosis for five years, would not be forced to suffer longer. I say emphatically that faith is not the power of positive thinking. Faith is not the personal resolve that enables us to *will* some difficult situation into being. Faith is not always the capacity to turn tragedy into celebration. Faith is a principle of power, of God's power. We do not generate faith on our own, for it is the gift of God (Ephesians 2:8). We do not act ourselves into faith, for faith is a gift of the Spirit (Moroni 10:11), given by God to suit his purposes and bless the body of Christ, the Church.

People act in faith when they act according to the will of God. To say that another way, I have sufficient faith to move a mountain to the middle of a lake only when I know that the Lord wants it moved! I have faith or power to touch the hearts of men and women with my testimony of the truth only when speaker and listener are prepared and readied for the delivery and receipt of the word. Even the Master could not perform miracles in the midst of a people steeped in spiritual indifference. "A prophet is not without honour," Jesus said in speaking of his own reception in Nazareth, "save in his own country, and in his own house. *And he did not many mighty works there because of their unbelief*" (Matthew 13:57–58; emphasis added). Similarly, the prophet-leader Mormon loved his people and poured out his soul in prayer in their behalf; "nevertheless, it was without faith, because of the hardness of their hearts" (Mormon 3:12). Someone watching from the sidelines, unaware of what faith really is, might have been tempted to cry out: "Come on, Mormon, where's your faith?"

Again, acting by faith is acting according to the will of the Lord. I remember very well one warm June evening in Louisiana, only a few months after I had returned from a mission, sitting with my mom and dad, watching television. The phone rang, and my father was quickly summoned to the hospital to give a priesthood blessing. A sixteen-year-old boy, a friend of my younger sister, had suddenly collapsed on the softball field and had been rushed to the hospital. My dad was told that he had been diagnosed with some strange degenerative nerve disease, and if something didn't happen soon he would die. We rushed to the hospital, took the elevator to the fifth floor, and hurried through the doors that opened into the waiting room. We were greeted by the sorrow and tears of a broken-hearted family—the young man had died. We did our best to console the mourners and then made our way home. As we walked in the back door my sister asked, "How is he?" I answered that her friend had passed away. She came right back with: "Well, why didn't you raise him from the dead?" Being the seasoned and experienced returned missionary that I was, having most all of the answers to life's questions, I stuttered for a second and then turned to my father: "Yeah, why didn't we raise him from the dead?" Dad's answer was kindly but firm. It was also terribly instructive: "Because the Spirit of the Lord didn't prompt us to do so," he said. In the years that followed, I came to know something about my dad's faith: he had been with his father once when in fact the Spirit had prompted and the dead had been raised to life again. He knew when to move and when not to move. He had faith. He knew how to exercise the priesthood faithfully.

Let me share another story. Wilford Woodruff was traveling to Zion to assume his new assignment to the Quorum of the Twelve (see D&C 118:6). On the journey his wife Phoebe was overcome with a high fever and lay at the point of death. "I alighted at a house," Brother Woodruff wrote, "and carried my wife and her bed into it, with a determination to tarry there until she either recovered her health or passed away. This was on Sunday morning, December 2nd. After getting my wife and things into the house and providing wood to keep up a fire, I employed my time in taking care of her. It looked as if she had but a short time to live. She called me to her bedside in the evening, and said she felt as if a few moments more would end her existence in this life. She manifested great confidence in the cause we had embraced, and exhorted me to have confidence in God, and to keep His commandments. To all appearances she was dying. I laid hands upon her and prayed for her, and she soon revived, and slept some during the night.

"December 3rd found my wife very low. I spent the day in taking care of her. . . . She seemed to be sinking gradually, and in the evening the spirit apparently left her body, and she was dead. The sisters gathered around, weeping, while I stood looking at her in sorrow. The spirit and power of God began to rest upon me until, for the first time during her sickness, faith filled my soul, although she lay before me as one dead.

"I had some oil that was consecrated for my anointing while in Kirtland. . . . I then bowed down before the Lord, prayed for the life of my companion, and in the name of the Lord I anointed her body with the oil. I then laid my hands upon her, and in the name of Jesus Christ I rebuked the power of death and of the destroyer, and commanded the same to depart from her and the spirit of life to enter her body. Her spirit returned to her body, and from that hour she was made whole; and we all felt to praise the name of God, and to trust in Him and to keep His commandments.

"While I was undergoing this ordeal (as my wife related afterwards) her spirit left her body, and she saw it lying upon the bed and the sisters there weeping. She looked at them and at me, and upon her babe; while gazing upon this scene, two persons came into the room . . . , and told her they had come for her. . . . One of these messengers said to her that she might have her choice—she might go to rest in the spirit world, or, upon one condition, she could have the privilege of returning to her tabernacle and of continuing her labors upon the earth. The condition was that if she felt that she could stand by her husband, and with him pass through all the cares, trials, tribulations, and afflictions of life which he would be called upon to pass through for the gospel's sake unto the end, she might return. When she looked at the situation of her husband and child she said, 'Yes, I will do it!' At the moment that decision was made the power of faith rested upon me, and when I administered unto her, her spirit reentered her tabernacle, and she saw the messengers [go out] the door" (Cowley, *Wilford Woodruff, His Life and Labors*, 96–98).

Joseph Smith taught that working by faith means working by the power of mental exertion rather than physical force (*Lectures on Faith,* 7:3). I am persuaded that the mental exertion of which he spoke is not merely a cognitive exercise, but rather a stern, strenuous effort, a spiritual search to know the will of God and then to accept and abide by that will. "Working by faith is not the mere speaking of a few well-chosen words," Elder Bruce R. McConkie has written; "anyone with the power of speech could have commanded the rotting corpse of Lazarus to come forth, but only one whose power was greater than death could bring life again to the brother of Mary and Martha. Nor is working by faith merely a mental desire, however strong, that some eventuality should occur. There may be those whose mental powers and thought processes are greater than any of the saints, but only persons who are in tune with the Infinite can exercise the spiritual forces and powers that come from him." In short, "Faith cannot be exercised contrary to the order of heaven or contrary to the will and purposes of him whose power it is. *Men work by faith when they are in tune with the Spirit and when what they seek to do by mental exertion and by the spoken word is the mind and will of the Lord*" (*A New Witness for the Articles of Faith,* 191–92; emphasis added).

The Lord asks us to move forward on the path of life on the basis of what has been made known through prophets. We cannot always see the end from the beginning. We cannot always act in the face of the observable or the demonstrable.

In many cases, believing must precede seeing. Indeed, the revelations affirm that as we "search diligently, pray always, and *be believing,* . . . all things shall work together for [our] good" (D&C 90:24; emphasis added). We are further counseled to doubt not because we see not, for we "receive no witness until after the trial of [our] faith" (Ether 12:6). This is the nature of the leap of faith, a leap from the safe and the secure to the anticipated and the hoped for (Alma 32:21). The disciples of Christ, and especially those who have been ordained and endowed with power from on high, are not called upon to proceed wholly in the dark, to leap from the precipice without evidence of deliverance. Rather, we are asked to rely upon the unseen, to trust in the quiet but persistent whisperings of the Spirit, to lean upon the prophetic promises. In the words of President Harold B. Lee, we must "learn to walk to the edge of the light, and perhaps a few steps into the darkness, and [we] will find that the light will appear and move ahead of [us]" (Cited in Packer, *The Holy Temple,* 184).

It is one thing to have the priesthood conferred upon us—to have the authority—and quite another to enjoy the power of the priesthood. The latter comes through worthiness, through enjoying the confirming presence of the Spirit (Moroni 3:4; D&C 18:32; 20:60; *Teachings of the Prophet Joseph Smith,* 323), inasmuch as "the rights of the priesthood are inseparably connected with the powers of heaven" and since "the powers of heaven cannot be controlled nor handled only upon the principles of righteousness" (D&C 121:36). It is a sobering responsibility to be ordained to God's own power and to be called upon to exercise it. We take our commission lightly at the peril of our salvation. At a time when many of the Saints in Nauvoo, Illinois, and Montrose, Iowa, were deathly ill, "Brother Joseph, while in the Spirit, rebuked the Elders who would continue to lay hands on the sick from day to day without the power to heal them. Said he: 'It is time that such things ended. Let the Elders either obtain the power of God to heal the sick, or let them cease to minister the forms without the power'" (*Autobiography of Parley P. Pratt*, 294).

No man who seeks for power in the priesthood can allow himself to "coast" spiritually through either distraction or preoccupation with lesser things; through becoming involved in immoral activities or in the wicked wave of pornography that now washes across our land like an apocalyptic plague; through acting the role of a vicious tyrant within his own home; or through disloyalty or evil speaking of the Lord's anointed servants. As holders of the priesthood and as covenant representatives, we are called to be the salt of the earth (Matthew 5:13; D&C 101:39–40). Elder Carlos E. Asay explained that "salt will not lose its savor with age. *Savor is lost through mixture and contamination.* . . .

"Flavor and quality flee a man when he contaminates his mind with unclean thoughts, desecrates his mouth by speaking less than the truth, and misapplies his strength in performing evil acts. . . .

"If it is not clean, do not think it; if it is not true, do not speak it; if it is not good, do not do it" (Conference Report, April 1980, 60; emphasis added).

Similarly, Elder John H. Groberg reminded us that "while the power *of* the priesthood is unlimited, our individual power *in* the priesthood is limited by our degree of righteousness or purity. . . .

"God, who is full of light, life, and love, wants us to hold and properly use His priesthood so we can transmit that light, life, and love to all about us. On the other hand, Satan, the prince of darkness, wants to hold back light, life, and love as much as he can. Since there is nothing Satan can do about the power *of* the priesthood, he concentrates his energy on trying to limit our individual power *in* the priesthood by attempting to dirty our hands, hearts, and minds. . . .

" . . . Remember, the sand castles we build on the beaches of mortality, no matter how elaborate, will eventually be washed away by the tide. Only purity of hand, heart, and mind will allow us to tap into the ultimate power of the priesthood to truly bless others and eventually be able to build eternal mansions more beautiful and lasting than we can presently imagine" (Conference Report, April 2001, 56, 58; emphasis in original).

The blessings of the priesthood do not come to us merely by "holding" divine authority; men are not called upon to hoard or monopolize its benefits. Rather, our task is to be willing and eager to share what we bear, to extend ourselves in righteous priesthood service, to "succor the weak, lift up the hands which hang down, and strengthen the feeble knees" (D&C 81:5). Many years ago while serving as a member of the bishopric, I attended with my two brethren a meeting that had been organized specifically for the women of the ward. The sisters stated that there were a number of issues they wanted to raise and questions they wanted to have us address. It was a pleasant and positive evening, and the questions posed were, for the most part, well thought through. Toward the end of the meeting, one sister asked a question that literally stunned me. She inquired: "What do we do when we ask our husbands to give us or our children a priesthood blessing but they refuse or are hesitant to do so?" There was a long pause. The members of the bishopric looked back and forth at one another, wondering who would venture forth with great wisdom. Finally, I blurted out: "Do you mean to say that you ask Dad to exercise his priesthood but he feels uncomfortable doing so?" She nodded in the affirmative. "Do any of the rest of you face the same challenge?" I asked. About fifty hands went up.

Now don't get me wrong. I knew the members of our ward well. I knew the men of the ward very well, and I considered them to be noble husbands and fathers. I couldn't think of too many exceptions, of brethren who weren't spiritually fit to serve or who were rebellious in any way. These women were hurting, yearning, longing for the men in their lives whom they loved to step up, move forward, and stand on higher ground. These women wanted to look to their husbands with respect and honor, to be able to say honestly that their spouses were men of God.

And yet there seemed to be among many of the brethren a kind of priesthood indifference, a spiritual inertia of sorts, a holding back, perhaps a shyness when it came to blessing (in more ways than healing) their loved ones. This must not be. Ours is the blessing to bless. Ours is the privilege of living in such a manner as to enjoy the love of God in our own souls and then extending that consummate endowment to others. "Love is one of the chief characteristics of Deity," Joseph Smith taught, "and ought to be manifested by those who aspire to be the sons of God. A man filled with the love of God, is not content with blessing his family alone, but ranges through the whole world, anxious to bless the whole human race" (*Teachings of the Prophet Joseph Smith*, 174).

To understand, at least to some degree, what we have within our grasp and within easy reach, is to understand that to be an elder of the Church is a pearl of great price. One who is ordained an elder holds all the Melchizedek Priesthood he will ever hold. To the response by one man that he was "only an elder," Elder McConkie replied: "*Only an elder!* Only the title by which a member of the Council of the Twelve is proud to be addressed; only the title which honors the President of the Church, who is designated by revelation as the first elder (see D&C 20:2, 5); only the office to which millions of persons are ordained in the vicarious ordinances of the holy temples.

"*Only an elder!* Only the office which enables a man to enter the new and everlasting covenant of marriage and to have his wife and children bound to him with an everlasting tie; only the office which prepares a man to be a natural patriarch to his posterity and to hold dominion in the house of Israel forever; only the office required for the receipt of the fullness of the blessings in the house of the Lord; only the office which opens the door to eternal exaltation in the highest heaven of the celestial world" ("Only an Elder," 66).

In late June of 2001 I suffered a massive heart attack while helping my son Jeff lay down sod in the front yard of his new home. It was a grueling and painful and disorienting experience, to be sure. While at the hospital my heart actually stopped, and so the doctors were required to drag out the paddles, just like they do on *E.R.*, and bring me back. I regret to inform the reader that I did not see a light, a tunnel, a being of light, or even find myself floating above my body; I didn't even get a decent near-death experience out of this! I did, however, obtain a new perspective on life and death, on priorities and people, on matters of primary and secondary importance. The first day in the hospital is all a blur to me now, except for the fact that my son Michael stayed with me all night, responding regularly to my plea for ice or water. By the second day I was thinking a little clearer, was in and out of consciousness, but felt as if I had been beaten up by a gang of thugs. By then the word had spread to my home ward and stake, my faculty colleagues, and the members of my BYU stake (I was serving as a stake president at the time), and so people had begun to come to the hospital to check on me in greater and greater numbers. Two of my sons, Jeff and David, chose to stand guard just outside the elevator to kindly ask any visitors to hold off for a few days. Then, without warning, the elevator doors opened and out stepped Elders Dallin H. Oaks and Joseph B. Wirthlin of the Quorum of the Twelve Apostles. My younger son Jeff essentially said to David, "We'd better tell these guys that visiting Dad is off limits and that they'll need to check back in a few days." David was a returned missionary, and so he recognized at once who the two distinguished-looking gentlemen were. He said something like, "No, I think we'd better let these two in to see Dad."

My sons accompanied the two General Authorities into my room. Elder Oaks, speaking for the two of them, said: "Brother Millet, we were down at the mission president's seminar at the MTC, and President Hinckley asked us to come by and check on you." I thanked them for coming and expressed how honored I was that they would make the effort. Elder Oaks asked: "Have you had a priesthood blessing yet?" I stated that my sons had blessed me, to which Elder Oaks responded: "Well, we don't have any more priesthood than they do. I'm certain you'll be just fine." And I was. This was not only a sweet experience for me but also a great learning moment for my sons. Being told that their priesthood blessing was just as potent as what I might receive from two Apostles was indeed a lesson of a lifetime for my boys. My sons were "only elders," but that was enough.

Only months before his death, President Harold B. Lee delivered a Brigham Young University devotional address. "One of our Latter-day Saint men during World War II was over in England," President Lee explained. "He had gone to an officer's club where they were holding a riotous kind of celebration. He noticed off to the side a young British officer who didn't seem to be enjoying himself at all. So he walked over to him and said, 'You don't seem to be enjoying this kind of a party.' And this young British officer straightened himself a few inches taller than he was before and replied, 'No, sir, I can't engage in this kind of party, because, you see, I belong to the royal household of England.'

"As our Latter-day Saint boy walked away he said to himself, 'Neither can I, because I belong to the royal household of the kingdom of God.' Do you realize that? . . . There are things that you cannot and must not do if you remember your heritage.

"I am reminded of the old court jester who was supposed to entertain his king with interesting stories and antics. He looked at the king who was lolling on his throne, a drunken, filthy rascal, doffed his cap and bells, and said with a mock gesture of obeisance, 'O king, be loyal to the royal within you.' And so I say to you . . . today, remember your heritage, and be loyal to that royal lineage that you have as members of the church and kingdom of God on the earth" ("Be Loyal to the Royal Within You," 100).

To repeat Peter's statement to the Saints scattered

abroad: "Ye are a chosen generation, a royal priesthood, an holy nation, *a peculiar people; that* ye should shew forth the praises of him who hath called you out of darkness into his marvellous light" (1 Peter 2:9; emphasis added). What does it mean to be peculiar? Does it mean odd, strange, or bizarre? Well, to some extent the Saints of the Most High are peculiar in the sense that we are different; we march to a different drummer and take our cues from a different source than the world. We stand up and speak out on issues or trends in our society that run contrary to the revealed word.

In that sense, the Church of the Lamb will almost always be a countercultural movement, a vote of opposition, a voice that proclaims soberly and certainly that we will not surrender to special-interest groups that seek to redefine marriage and the family or that contribute to the erosion of time-honored values like chastity and virtue. If it be thought odd to stand where the former-day Saints have stood on issues of decency, then so be it; we will be odd. If it be thought weird to deny and defy the immodesty of our day and even establish a style of our own, then so be it; we will be weird. If it be thought bizarre or naïve for a husband and father to be true to his covenants and stand boldly against marital infidelity, then so be it; we will be bizarre and naïve.

But there is a deeper meaning intended by Peter: the word translated as *peculiar* could be rendered as *purchased.* We are a purchased people. We are not our own; we have been bought with a price. We have been redeemed by the precious blood of the Master (1 Corinthians 6:19; 7:23). While once we had sold ourselves by our sins (Isaiah 50:1), we have been bought back "with the precious blood of Christ, as of a lamb without blemish and without spot" (1 Peter 1:19). The worth of souls is thus great in the sight of God, "for, behold, the Lord your Redeemer suffered death in the flesh; wherefore he suffered the pain of all men, that all men might repent and come unto him. And he hath risen again from the dead, that he might bring all men unto him, on conditions of repentance. And how great is his joy in the soul that repenteth!" (D&C 18:11–13).

Alma taught the wicked men and women of Ammonihah that all those who receive the Melchizedek Priesthood in this life were foreordained to receive the same in the premortal realm (Alma 13:3–5). Joseph the Prophet likewise declared that "every man who has a calling to minister to the inhabitants of the world was ordained to that very purpose in the Grand Council of heaven before this world was" (*Teachings of the Prophet Joseph Smith,* 365). In other words, we have been *called* from the foundation of the world. The questions before us are: Will I magnify my callings within the Holy Priesthood after the Order of the Son of God? Will I trust in and rely upon the merits and mercy and grace of that Holy Messiah, so as to open the heavens and draw freely upon his divine enabling power? Will I seek to emulate my Priesthood Prototype and thereby become *chosen* to receive all that our Father has? The answers to these questions lie deep within each of our hearts. We are heirs to the blessings of heavenly royalty. To the extent that we honor the divine authority granted unto us, then Jesus the Christ will redeem us "to God by [his] blood out of every kindred, and tongue, and people, and nation; and [will make] us unto our God kings and priests: and we shall reign on the earth" (Revelation 5:9–10).

POINTS TO PONDER

1. What does it mean to exercise faith in the divine purposes of our Heavenly Father? Why is it necessary for me to have faith in Jesus the Christ?

2. Let's suppose that I have been asked by God to move a mountain. What is the difference between what I feel when I walk up to the mountain to move it, and what I feel when I walk away from the mountain having moved it? What does this brief exercise suggest about the nature of faith?

3. What is the difference between true faith and the power of positive thinking? Joseph Smith is reported to have taught that when we work by faith we work by the power of mental exertion (*Lectures on Faith*, 7:3). What does this mean?

4. How prone would my colleagues or friends of other faiths be to call me a peculiar person? What would help them to understand that I have in fact come to be a peculiar person, a man of the priesthood who has chosen to take the road less traveled?

ACTING IN HIS NAME

IN THE PRECEDING CHAPTERS we have spoken briefly about the privileges and burdens associated with holding the priesthood, about what it means to "rise up" as a man of God and be a "mighty man of valor." The gospel of Jesus Christ—including especially the scriptures, ancient and modern—set forth what it really means to be a man. The world has its own models and ideals, but God himself, a glorified, exalted Man of Holiness (Moses 6:57), has delivered to us a pattern, a template, a design by which those called and chosen to bear the holy priesthood may become "men of Christ." In the 1950s certain TV commercials spoke of the "Marlboro man." People today often refer to themselves as a "Harvard man" or a "Stanford man," meaning of course that these men seek to be identified with the brand of cigarettes they smoke or the university from which they graduated. What a delight it would be one day to hear our children or grandchildren refer to you and me as "a priesthood man" or "a man of Christ." Whether or not these terms apply to us will depend entirely upon the life we live, the image we portray, and how we structure our eternal priorities.

Mormon reminded us that "the Lord is merciful unto all who will, in the sincerity of their hearts, call upon *his holy name*. Yea, thus we see that the gate of heaven is open unto all, even to those who will *believe on the name of Jesus Christ*, who is the Son of God. Yea, we see that whosoever will may lay hold upon the word of God, which is quick and powerful, which shall divide asunder all the cunning and the snares and the wiles of the devil, and lead *the man of Christ* in a strait and narrow course across that everlasting gulf of misery which is prepared to engulf the wicked—and land their souls, yea, their immortal souls, at the right hand of God in the kingdom of heaven, to sit down with Abraham, and Isaac, and with Jacob, and with all our holy fathers, to go no more out" (Helaman 3:27–30; emphasis added).

As we have suggested before, a priesthood man, a man of Christ, is one who chooses to do things the Lord's way, one who determines to yield his heart unto God and thereby enjoy the sanctifying influence that flows therefrom (Helaman 3:35; D&C 84:33). In 1982 my family and I were asked by the Church Educational System to relocate from Tallahassee, Florida, to Athens, Georgia, in order to assume a new responsibility. I had completed course work for my doctoral degree at Florida State University, but because the experience was so exhausting, I had not given serious attention to my dissertation for almost a year. Only three weeks after we had settled in Athens, I received a phone call from a member of the search committee in Religious Education at Brigham Young University. He indicated that I was on a short list of candidates for hiring and wanted to know simply if I were interested in being considered seriously. I stated that I loved BYU and would be honored to be a part of the faculty there. I was then asked: "Is there any question, Bob, that you will be finished with your dissertation by a year from now?" I thought about the task before me and responded quickly: "None whatsoever." I began work on the dissertation that day!

I did not hear much from BYU in the next several months and often wondered where things were in the selection process. Shauna had been born and raised in Utah, and the possibility of living closer to her family was exciting to her. I had loved my religion classes at the "Y" and felt it would be thrilling to teach there. But no word came. We prayed and prayed and prayed. We fasted and prayed and prayed. But no word came. In essence, our prayers consisted of the following sentiments (although we would certainly never have said these exact words): "Heavenly Father, we would love to go to BYU and feel like we could make a contribution to the kingdom in Provo. Would you please, please, please bring it to pass?" This went on from August until early March, until we were, to be honest, nervous wrecks.

I happened to be in Tallahassee one weekend to work with my dissertation advisor when I met my old stake president, Richard Chapple. I had served as a bishop under him and had the consummate privilege also of being called to work with him in the stake presidency. He was my model of a priesthood man, a man of Christ, one of the greatest examples of a priesthood leader I have known; I could write volumes on what he taught me in only five years about the worth of souls and the work of the kingdom. He asked how things were going and specifically what I had heard from Religious Education at BYU. I said that we had not heard much, but that we wanted the position desperately. He looked at me in an odd way and said: "It means that much to you?" I nodded affirmatively. "Haven't I taught you better than this?" he asked. "What do you mean?" I followed up. "Bob," he said, "you know and I know that we are engaged in the work of the Lord, and that it just doesn't matter where we are serving, as long as we are where the Lord wants us to be. Now quit worrying about it and turn it all over to Him. When it doesn't matter to you anymore where you work or how you serve, God will answer your prayers and put you where you can do the greatest good."

At first I felt as if his counsel was the dumbest thing I had ever heard (although I didn't let on that I felt that way). I later discussed the conversation with Shauna. As we thought about it, we both felt a bit chastened by his words and found ourselves repenting of selfishness and praying more regularly: "Father in Heaven, we just want to be where we ought to be. Is that place Athens, Georgia? Then we're prepared and eager to stay here. Is it Provo, Utah? Then we're happy to go there. Please, just let us know one way or the other." A short time later the phone rang, I was invited to Provo for a set of interviews, and eventually I was offered a job there. But in all earnestness I can say that by that point my wife and I were just as ready to stay where we were, to sink our roots in Georgia, and to make whatever contribution we could. That change of heart did not come overnight, but it did come. We prayed for the Lord to empower us, to enable us—to grant unto us his divine grace—so that we might say, "Thy will be done" and mean it (D&C 109:44). A priesthood man, a man of Christ, has no private agenda; rather, as an agent he seeks to know the will of his Principal and pleads for the strength and capacity to carry it out.

Further, one holding God's power must learn to speak and act properly when he functions in the name of Deity. In a world where upright and moral, God-fearing people would never even conceive of murder or theft or adultery, it is surprising how often the name of God is taken in vain without a second thought. Even among those in our society who are civic-minded and service-oriented, we too often hear the sacred name of Deity dragged through the gutter through being placed in an alien context—through flippant, profane, or unclean speech. Why is it that good people can be so observant of those Sinaitic commandments that pertain to interpersonal relationships but miss the mark of propriety in regard to the sanctity that should attend the name and person of the Almighty?

Taking the name of God in vain entails far more than profaning his name, more than cursing and blaspheming. It of course has something to do with the way we speak, but, more important, it has to do with *the way we live and the way we are.* It has to do with our eternal perspective, with the manner in which we think and act upon sacred things. It has everything to do with the way we assume our covenantal responsibilities as Christians. As holders of the holy priesthood, we have been called by prophecy and by the laying on of hands (Articles of Faith 1:5) to bear this divine authority, to live our lives in a manner that would bring dignity and respect to the sacred name of Deity and would allow the powers of godliness to flow freely into our lives.

There is a name that is above every other name that is named, whether on earth or in heaven, save only the name of the Almighty Elohim (Philippians 2:9–11). There is a name that brings joy to the desolate heart, a name that speaks peace to the sorrowing soul. There is a name that falls in hushed and hallowed tones from the lips of saints and angels, a name that leads true believers on both sides of the veil to glory and honor everlasting. It is the name of the One sent of God to bring salvation, the name of the One who paid the infinite price to ransom us from Satan's grasp. It is the blessed name of Jesus Christ.

An angel explained to father Adam nearly six millennia

ago: "*Thou shalt do all that thou doest in the name of the Son,* and thou shalt repent and call upon God in the name of the Son forevermore" (Moses 5:8; emphasis added). We are to do all things in the name of the Son. *All* things. We are to speak and act and worship and perform the labors of the kingdom—all in the name of the Son. We are the servants of the Lord, who is our Master, and he has commanded us to labor in his fields—plowing, sowing, cultivating, and harvesting. That is, we are the *agents* of the Lord, who is our eternal *Principal,* and he has empowered us to represent him, to do the things he would do if he were personally present. To do all things in his name in righteousness means that we put ourselves in his place and stead, that we open ourselves to the Spirit so as to be able to think and speak and act as though we were the One whose blessed name we bear. Our acts become his acts—they are done in his name and by his authority.

It is an awesome responsibility to speak in the name of the Lord. The messengers of salvation are under obligation to "declare the word with truth and soberness" (Alma 42:31). That is, they are to be faithful to the spirit and intent of the message to be delivered. Nephi explained that those who speak under the influence of the Spirit speak "with the tongue of angels"; they declare what angels would declare if they were present. Such persons thereby speak "the words of Christ" (2 Nephi 31:13; 32:1–3). While the apostles and prophets stand as the examples and models of what all the Saints of the Most High should be and do in this regard, the everlasting gospel has been restored in our day "that *every man* might speak in the name of God the Lord, even the Savior of the world" (D&C 1:20; emphasis added).

God the Eternal Father has placed his name upon the Son (see John 5:43; 10:25). Thus, in using his Father's name, Jesus made his words and acts those of his Father. There are numerous places in scripture in which Jesus speaks in behalf of his Father in the first person, as though he were the Almighty Elohim, using the very words of his Father. His doing so is an illustration of speaking by divine investiture of authority. Men and women who have been ordained or set apart to deliver the message of salvation—who have been commissioned to represent the Lord and proclaim the truths of his everlasting gospel—likewise may speak by divine investiture of authority. They do not necessarily declare, "Thus saith the Lord," and it is not necessary that they speak in the first person for the Father or for Jesus Christ his Son. But they do stand as representatives and agents of their Master and as such are entitled to the quiet yet persuasive whisperings of the Holy Spirit, which, when they receive them, authorize and justify their utterances. God honors his servants. He vindicates the words of his chosen vessels (see Moses 6:32–34).

That Jesus performed ordinances is well known. He baptized, conferred the Holy Ghost, administered the sacrament, ordained men to priestly offices—all in the power and authority of his divine Sonship. But he is not available to do these things for each individual, so he empowers others to act in his name—he extends an investiture of authority, if you will—to ensure that all have the privilege of receiving those powers and rites that enable us to become even as he is. To be valid, all ordinances must be performed by him or by his word—meaning, by his servants who act in his holy name. Thus the former-day Saints rejoiced that the power of God was theirs, so that when they stretched forth their hand in faith it became the hand of the Almighty (see Acts 4:30). Similarly, in a revelation given through the Prophet Joseph Smith to Edward Partridge, "the Lord God, the Mighty One of Israel," said: "*I will lay my hand upon you by the hand of my servant Sidney Rigdon,* and you shall receive my Spirit, the Holy Ghost, even the Comforter, which shall teach you the peaceable things of the kingdom" (D&C 36:1–2; emphasis added).

As it is with the performance of ordinances, so it is in regard to the working of miracles. Jesus came in his Father's name, but he also came in his own right, and when he performed miracles he acted in all the majesty of his own divine calling. He healed the sick and forgave sins; in so doing, he illustrated his power over both physical and spiritual maladies (see JST Matthew 9:1–5; compare JST Luke 5:23). Jesus is God, and God works miracles in his own right; he needs neither the name nor the power of another. In contrast, all those who are agents of the Lord act and operate and are authorized by the name above all other names, the name of our Savior (see Ephesians 3:15; Philippians 2:9).

Even as an exalted and resurrected being, our Lord continued to pray to his Father, sometimes praying in words of such spiritual grandeur that they could not be repeated or written (see 3 Nephi 17:13–17; 19:31–36). We are commanded to pattern our prayers after his. Further, we are commanded to pray to the Father in the name of the Son. Our prayers do not go through the Son to the Father, for we are commanded to "come boldly unto the throne of grace" (Hebrews 4:16; compare Moses 7:59). Rather, we are entitled to address the Father directly, because of the Son—by virtue of his ministry of reconciliation, his advocacy of our cause, and his intercession on our behalf (see Alma 33:8–11, 16; D&C 45:3–5). But there is more. We are to pray in the name of Jesus Christ. What does that mean? Is it not the same as with preaching and prophesying and performing ordinances and miracles? All of these are done in his name. When we pray in Christ's name, among other things, we seek to put ourselves in his place and stead. We say the words he would say, because our prayers, when they meet the divine standard, are spoken by the power of the Holy Spirit. And because they are spoken in the name of the blessed Jesus, our words become his words; they are what he would say in the same situation. Truly, "he that asketh in the Spirit asketh according to the will of God; wherefore it is done even as he asketh" (D&C 46:30; see also Helaman 10:5).

How then does one become guilty of taking the name of

God in vain, whether it be the name of the Father or of the Son?

1. *Through profanity and vulgarity.* The most commonly understood violation is in regard to speaking the name of Deity in the context of cursing or profaning. It is interesting to note that the word *profane* means literally "outside the temple." What a poignant way to describe the profanation of the name of God: to take that which is most holy, to remove it from its hallowed setting, and to thrust it into an environment that is unholy and unclean. Thus alternate translations of this passage read as follows: "You must not make wrong use of the name of the Lord your God" (Revised English Bible); "You shall not make wrongful use of the name of the Lord your God" (New Revised Standard Version); "You shall not misuse the name of the Lord your God" (New International Version). President Gordon B. Hinckley taught: "So serious was violation of this law considered in ancient Israel that blasphemy of the name of the Lord was regarded as a capital crime. . . .

"While that most serious of penalties has long since ceased to be inflicted, the gravity of the sin has not changed" (Conference Report, October 1987, 56).

The growing amount of profanity and vulgarity in music, books, television, the motion picture industry, and the Internet merely serves as a commentary on our times. It just may be that people's inhumanity to people is not unrelated to their neglect of sacred matters, that the growing harshness, crudeness, and insensitivity in society are correlated directly with denying, defying, and ignoring God. Our speech too often betrays us; it shows what and who we are. One who loves the Lord, cherishes his word, and bows beneath his rod seeks always to act and speak with deferential reverence toward Deity. On the other hand, one who knows not God and who finds no personal value in worship or devotion has no meaningful concept of the Holy or of holiness. For such persons there may be no sense of restraint in their speech, no hesitation to lift the sacred out of its context and thrust it into the profane.

In a modern revelation, the Lord declared: "Behold, *I am from above,* and my power lieth beneath. I am over all, and in all, and through all, and search all things, and the day cometh that all things shall be subject unto me. Behold, I am Alpha and Omega, even Jesus Christ. Wherefore, *let all men beware how they take my name in their lips*—for behold, verily I say, that *many there be who are under this condemnation, who use the name of the Lord, and use it in vain, having not authority. . . .* Remember that *that which cometh from above is sacred, and must be spoken with care, and by constraint of the Spirit;* and in this there is no condemnation" (D&C 63:59–62, 64; emphasis added). The Lord is from above, as is his word and his priesthood power. When we speak of him or take his name, we should and must do so with the deepest reverence. To do otherwise is to take or hold up or raise up his holy name before others without serious thought, without appropriate reflection, in vain.

Elder Dallin H. Oaks thus explained that "we take the name of the Lord in vain when we use his name without authority. This obviously occurs when the sacred names of God the Father and his Son, Jesus Christ, are used in what is called profanity: in hateful cursings, in angry denunciations, or as marks of punctuation in common discourse." On the other hand, Elder Oaks added, "The names of the Father and the Son are used with authority when we reverently teach and testify of them, when we pray, and when we perform the sacred ordinances of the priesthood" (Conference Report, April 1986, 66).

2. *Through the breaking of oaths and covenants.* To ancient Israel the Lord said: "Ye shall not swear by my name falsely, neither shalt thou profane the name of thy God; I am the Lord" (Leviticus 19:12). As one commentator has written: "This prohibition applies strictly to perjury or false swearing, the breaking of a promise or contract that has been sealed with an oath in the name of God. He will not allow His name to be associated with any act of falsehood or treachery. His name must not be taken in vain, i.e., lightly or heedlessly" (Dummelow, *One Volume Bible Commentary,* 67).

Without truth there can be no society, no order among men and women. Anciently an oath was a means of impressing the necessity of truth and integrity upon parties to an agreement or upon witnesses in an investigation. That obligation was fortified by holy words and sacred acts intended to bring a sense of confidence and assurance to those involved. Thus the legal procedure, of which an oath was a part, was administered by persons and sealed by the invocation of the name of Deity. To perjure such an oath was indeed a very serious matter and was not to go unpunished (see Ezekiel 17:13, 16, 18–19). In time people began to abuse the oath, to swear in a manner that was unholy, inappropriate, or that would allow for loopholes. Jesus thus called his followers to a greater accountability: "Swear not at all," he said, "neither by heaven; for it is God's throne: nor by the earth; for it is his footstool: neither by Jerusalem; for it is the city of the great King. Neither shalt thou swear by thy head, because thou canst not make one hair white or black. But let your communication be, Yea, yea; Nay, nay: for whatsoever is more than these cometh of evil" (Matthew 5:34–37). His was a call to a higher righteousness, a call to his disciples to let their word be their bond. If one says "Yes" as a part of a legal or interpersonal arrangement, then mean "Yes." If one says "No," then mean "No." Personal honor and integrity are at stake.

Covenants are two-way promises between us and our God. All gospel covenants and ordinances are administered and entered into in the name of Jesus Christ. Nothing can be done for the salvation of humankind in any other name or by any other authority. The composite of "all covenants, contracts, bonds, obligations, oaths, vows, performances, connections, associations, or expectations" constitutes the new and everlasting covenant (D&C 132:6–7; compare 1:22; 45:9; 66:2). To willingly or knowingly violate the terms of our covenants or any of the component parts—including the oath and covenant of the Melchizedek Priesthood (D&C 84:33–44)—is thus to take the name of the Lord in vain: to take lightly, treat as empty and meaningless our sacred and solemn obligations. God will not be mocked (Galatians 6:7), nor will he suffer that his holy ordinances be treated capriciously or cavalierly. The gravity of sin is in proportion to the understanding of the transgressor. Truly, "For of him unto whom much is given much is required; and he who sins against the greater light shall receive the greater condemnation" (D&C 82:3; compare 63:66; Luke 12:48). "Hearken and hear, O ye my people, saith the Lord and your God, ye whom I delight to bless with the greatest of all blessings, ye that hear me; and *ye that hear me not will I curse, that have professed my name*, with the heaviest of all cursings" (D&C 41:1; emphasis added). The Lord has warned that in the last days vengeance will come speedily upon the inhabitants of the earth. "And upon my house shall it begin, and from my house shall it go forth, saith the Lord; *first among those among you, saith the Lord, who have professed to know my name and have not known me*, and have blasphemed against me in the midst of my house, saith the Lord" (D&C 112:24–26; emphasis added).

3. *Through being flippant, sacrilegious, and irreverent.* Several years ago a young man addressed our ward in sacrament

meeting. He said, in essence: "Brothers and sisters, it's great to be in your ward today. I am told that the best way to get a congregation with you is to liven them up with a few jokes." He related several humorous stories, at least a couple of which were inappropriate for the occasion. He then began to do impersonations of the president of the United States, indicating what it would be like if the president were to take the missionary discussions. The congregation roared. At least some of them did. Some sat in stupor. Others, like myself, wondered what was going on. After fifteen or twenty minutes, the young man looked at his watch and said, "Well, I'd better close now. I say all these things in the name of Jesus Christ. Amen."

His address was amusing, entertaining, something that might be fun to witness in a road show or a youth activity or a family home evening. But we were in a sacrament meeting, one of the sacred worship services of The Church of Jesus Christ of Latter-day Saints. There was something haunting about the words, "In the name of Jesus Christ." I had, of course, heard those very words at least ten thousand times over the years. But that day it was different. I became very introspective. I thought of all the times I had delivered talks or offered prayers or administered to the sick in the name of Jesus Christ, but had done so without much reflection upon whose name I had taken. I thought of occasions where I had spoken on topics of my own choosing, but topics that may not have represented what the Lord wanted discussed. I thought of those times I had closed my prayers in a flash, zipping through the name of the Redeemer as though I were sprinting toward some finish line. I thought of the scores of times I had partaken of the emblems of the body and blood of the Savior with my mind focused on things alien to the spirit of the occasion.

It occurred to me then, and has many times since, that one need not be involved with profanity in order to be guilty of taking the name of the Lord our God in vain. He or she needs merely to treat lightly, flippantly, and without serious thought the sobering charge we carry as members of the Church of Jesus Christ to speak and act in God's name. We are a happy people, and the joy and satisfaction that derive from living the gospel must not be kept a secret. On the other hand, Joseph Smith taught that "the things of God are of deep import; and time, and experience, and careful and ponderous and solemn thoughts can only find them out" (*Teachings of the Prophet Joseph Smith*, 137).

Our reverence for life—our appreciation for the earth and for all things on its surface, especially human beings—is inextricably tied to our reverence for God. To draw close to Divinity is to come to appreciate man as a divine creation, for "If men do not comprehend the character of God, they do not comprehend themselves" (*Teachings of the Prophet Joseph Smith*, 343). Truly, "the nearer man approaches perfection, the clearer are his views, and the greater his enjoyments" (*Teachings of the Prophet Joseph Smith*, 51). Civilizations that have fallen—whether Greek or Roman or Nephite or Jaredite—are often characterized as a people who were "without order and without mercy," "without principle," and "past feeling" (see Moroni 9:18, 20). Those, on the other hand, who have transcended this fallen world—for example, the righteous societies of old—were peoples who were possessed of great spiritual sensitivity, who were impelled by a quest for the holiness of God, and who reverenced his name and the works of his hands. Having come unto God in the appointed ways, they in time were endowed with the greatest of all the fruits of the Spirit: their pure love for God motivated a pure love for their brothers and sisters (see Moroni 7:45–48; see also Galatians 5:22–25). They came to be known as Zion—a holy commonwealth where every man sought the interest of his neighbor and did all things with an eye single to the glory of God (see D&C 82:19).

To treat God, or that which properly bears his name, with disdain or contempt or even indifference cannot be less than a serious sin. That which profanes the sacred may be born of ignorance, disbelief, or hypocrisy. In any case, it is offensive to the spirit of light and truth; it is attractive to the spirit of darkness and error. Each spirit brings with it its own train of attendants. "That which is of God is light; and he that receiveth light, and continueth in God, receiveth more light; and that light groweth brighter and brighter until the perfect day" (see D&C 50:24). Those whose "minds have been darkened by unbelief" because they have "treated lightly" the manifestations of heaven are "under condemnation"; theirs is the promise of a scourge and judgment, for they have profaned the sacred (see D&C 84:54–59).

To be called upon to speak or act in the name of God is a sacred trust. It is deserving of solemn and ponderous thought. One wonders if we would not preach more gospel doctrines and bear more fervent testimonies if we had fixed in our minds the weighty fact that the words spoken or the deeds done are not ours alone, but they are the words and actions of our eternal Principal. And if there are times when we speak or act or pray without seeking for inspiration, if we teach for doctrine the views and philosophies of men, if we act or perform anything flippantly or lightly—and do it all in the name of the Lord—at such times, one wonders whether we are not taking the name of God in vain.

Jesus, as the supreme agent of our Heavenly Father, was engaged in his Father's business. We have a like appointment, and our divine commission includes the sobering provision we quoted earlier: "Wherefore, as ye are agents, ye are on the Lord's errand; and whatsoever ye do according to the will of the Lord is the Lord's business" (D&C 64:29). As President Spencer W. Kimball counseled: "It is not enough to refrain from profanity or blasphemy. We need to make important in our lives the name of the Lord. While we do not use the Lord's name lightly, we should not leave our friends or our neighbors or our children in any doubt as to where we stand. Let there be no doubt about our being followers of Jesus

Christ" (Conference Report, October 1978, 7). We are counseled by Him who is Eternal: "Take upon you the name of
Christ, and speak the truth in soberness" (D&C 18:21).

The Lord's people should rejoice in him and sing praises
unto his holy name continually. When we think of what has
been revealed in this day in regard to the Holy One of Israel;
when we ponder upon the light and truth and priesthood
power that have been delivered in this final dispensation of
grace; when we reflect upon the fact that living oracles—
apostles and prophets, special witnesses of the name of
Christ in all the world (D&C 107:23)—walk the earth today;
when we consider that holy temples—hallowed edifices upon
which God has placed his name and in which the covenants
and ordinances associated with eventually having the name
of God sealed upon our foreheads forever may be received—
are dotting the earth, our souls should well up with eternal
gratitude. Truly our cup is full. Our desires to acknowledge,
recognize, and praise him who is eternal should know no
bounds.

With a fervor and zeal born of the Spirit, and one which
we might well emulate, the Psalmist proclaimed: "O Lord
[Jehovah] our Lord, how excellent is thy name in all the earth!
who hast set thy glory above the heavens" (Psalm 8:1). The
Apostle Paul counseled the Corinthians: "Know ye not that
ye are the temple of God, and that the Spirit of God dwelleth
in you? If any man defile the temple of God, him shall God
destroy; for the temple of God is holy, which temple ye are"

(1 Corinthians 3:16–17; see also 6:19–20). Being true to what and who we are thus entails embodying a divine principle, a principle that adorns and identifies sacred edifices throughout the earth, a principle that also identifies the people of God, particularly those ordained to act in his name: "Holiness to the Lord."

In speaking of the ancients, the patriarchs, the holy word attests: "Now this same priesthood, which was in the beginning, shall be in the end of the world also" (Moses 6:7). What was true for the ancients is true for us. We hold the same priesthood held by Adam and Enoch and Noah and Melchizedek and Abraham and Moses and Peter and John and Paul. What inspired and motivated them can and should entice us to continuing fidelity and devotion to our covenants. The same authority by which they were baptized, confirmed, endowed, married, and sealed unto eternal life— that same authority has been delivered to earth in our day by heavenly messengers. Having come into the family of the Lord Jesus Christ by adoption (see Mosiah 5:7), we come to be known as the seed of Abraham, children and thus heirs of the Abrahamic covenant (Galatians 3:27–29; 2 Nephi 30:2; D&C 84:34). We are charged, as President Harold B. Lee stated (and as quoted in the last chapter) to "be loyal to the royal within us." Such is our opportunity and our great challenge, our glory or our condemnation.

POINTS TO PONDER

1. Would my wife or my children have any hesitation identifying me as a priesthood man or a man of Christ? What obstacles should be removed from my life in order for me to claim and be worthy of such titles?

2. What is involved in a complete surrender of my will and agency to God? What things in daily life tend to get in the way of such an unconditional surrender?

3. What does it mean to speak and act in the name of the Lord? How does a realization of what is involved in this sobering experience affect what I choose to do and what I choose not to do, what I choose to say and what I choose not to say?

4. In our own day we have witnessed the partial fulfillment of the prophecy that temples of the Lord will dot the earth. Each such sacred edifice contains a phrase that is pregnant with poignancy: "Holiness to the Lord." Since the prophets have taught us that we as children of the covenant, and particularly bearers of God's holy priesthood, are in fact the temples of the Lord (see 1 Corinthians 3:16–17; 6:19–20), am I living in a manner that would indeed manifest divine holiness? What must I do in order to become a holy man, a priesthood man, a man of Christ?

CONCLUSION

LATTER-DAY SAINTS DO NOT have a monopoly on goodness, a lock on the focus on families, or even a corner on a feeling of divine call to make a difference in our suffering society. Thank heavens for the fact that noble men and women throughout the earth remain true to their consciences, faithful to what we have come to know as the Judeo-Christian ethic, obedient to the laws and ordinances of decency that are foundational to any society that desires to succeed and leave a legacy in the world.

In January of 1982 at Washington's National Airport, Air Florida's Flight 90 to Tampa crashed into the 14th Street Bridge and slid into the Potomac River with seventy-four passengers aboard. One reporter explained: "For a moment, there was silence, and then pandemonium. Commuters watched helplessly as the plane quickly sank. . . . A few passengers bobbed to the surface; some clung numbly to pieces of debris while others screamed desperately for help. Scattered across the ice were pieces of green upholstery, twisted chunks of metal, luggage, a tennis racket, a child's shoe. . . .

"Within minutes, sirens began to wail as fire trucks, ambulances and police cars rushed to the scene. A U.S. Park Police helicopter hovered overhead to pluck survivors out of the water. Six were clinging to the plane's tail. Dangling a life preserving ring to them, the chopper began ferrying them to shore. One woman had injured her right arm, so [the pilot] . . . lowered the copter until its skids touched the water; his partner [then leaped out and] scooped her up in his arms. . . . Then [a young woman] grabbed the preserver, but as she was being helped out of the icy river by [a] fellow passenger, she lost her grip. . . . A clerk for the Congressional Budget Office who was watching from the shore, plunged into the water and dragged her to land. But the most notable act of heroism was performed by [another] of the passengers, a balding man in his early 50s. Each time the ring was lowered, he grabbed it and passed it along to a comrade; when the helicopter finally returned to pick him up, he had disappeared beneath the ice" (Kelly, "We're Not Going to Make It," 16–17).

In that same issue of *Time,* another writer described the unknown man in the water: "His selflessness [is] one reason the story held national attention; his anonymity another. The fact that he [has gone] unidentified invests him with a universal character. . . . For a while he was Everyman, and thus proof (as if one needed it) that no man is ordinary.

"Still, he could never have imagined such a capacity in

himself. Only minutes before his character was tested, he was sitting in the ordinary plane among the ordinary passengers, dutifully listening to the stewardess telling him to fasten his seat belt and saying something about the 'no smoking sign.' So our man relaxed with the others, some of whom would owe their lives to him. Perhaps he started to read, or to doze, or to regret some harsh remark made in the office that morning. Then suddenly he knew that the trip would not be ordinary. Like every other person on that flight, he was desperate to live, which makes his final act so stunning.

"For at some moment in the water he must have realized that he would not live if he continued to hand over the rope and ring to others. He had to know it, no matter how gradual the effect of the cold. In his judgment he had no choice. When the helicopter took off with what was to be the last survivor, he watched everything in the world move away from him, and he deliberately let it happen. . . .

"The odd thing is that we do not . . . really believe that the man in the water lost his fight. . . . He could not [like Nature] make ice storms, or freeze the water until it froze the blood. But he could hand life over to a stranger, and that is a power of nature too. The man in the water pitted himself against an implacable, impersonal enemy; he fought it with charity; and he [won]" (Rosenblatt, "The Man in the Water," 86).

Now this man was not a Latter-day Saint, nor do we know if he was a Christian. But we do know this—he was a good man, a sensitive soul, a caring human being who placed the needs of others before his own, and in this case it cost him his life. Some things mattered more to him than life and death. Some things transcended comfort and convenience and security and prosperity. And survival. Something deep down inside him drove him to live the Golden Rule (Matthew 7:12), to fulfill the Royal Law, the Law of Christ (James 2:8; compare Galatians 5:14; 6:2). Something within his being impelled him to put off the natural man that seeks its own gratification and rise to that nobility that mirrors the life and ministry of Jesus the Christ, the Prince of Peace.

Those called to bear the holy priesthood are charged to be constant and consistent, to be tender and teachable, to be loyal and loving. Few of us are called upon to move mountains or part the Red Sea, but we are called upon to establish peace in our homes, to be examples of the believer at our places of work, and to live in such a manner that our words and deeds become the words and deeds of Him who has called us. Like the early Apostles, we are ordained to bring forth fruit and told that our fruit should remain (John 15:16). We have enlisted in the Army of Jehovah and committed to follow him into the battle for the souls of our brothers and sisters. While we speak of the priesthood as that which has been delegated to mortal men, we must never forget that it is in fact *the power of God*—the power by which worlds came rolling into existence, the power by which all things were created and made, the power by which the inhabitants of those worlds are baptized, confirmed, ordained, endowed, redeemed, married for eternity, sealed up unto eternal life, and glorified hereafter.

This is the power we hold. We receive it with sobriety, for it is sacred. We accept it with humility, for it is solemn. We hallow it, for it is, like the Exalted Person who confers it, holy. Indeed, while one does not need the priesthood of God to do good deeds or even to read and study and teach the holy word, one must have had this privilege and this honor conferred upon him in order to lead the Lord's people in His way, perform and oversee the ordinances of salvation, and qualify to stand in that celestial day as a king and a priest after the order of Melchizedek, which is after the Order of the Son of God (D&C 76:56–57). The holy priesthood is an endowment of power, mercifully given to train us in the ways of godliness, to tutor us in the pattern of divine service and government, to prepare us to rule and reign in the worlds ahead as the covenant seed of Abraham, Isaac, and Jacob. It is what equips us to mature spiritually, to grow up in the Lord, to become mighty men of valor. Its institution is from before the foundation of the world, and its influence will be infinite and eternal. God be praised for the priesthood!

REFERENCES

Asay, Carlos. Conference Report, April 1980, 59–62.

Ballard, M. Russell. Conference Report, October 2005, 42–46.

Benson, Ezra Taft. Conference Report, April 1988, 2–6.

Clark, J. Reuben, Jr. "Spiritual and Temporal Rehabilitation," *Improvement Era,* November 1948, 730–31. Cited in Hinckley, *The Teahcings of Gordon B. Hinckley,* 488.

Cowley, Matthias F. *Wilford Woodruff, His Life and Labors.* Salt Lake City: Deseret News, 1916.

Crabb, Larry. *Inside Out.* Rev. ed. Colorado Springs, Colo.: NavPress, 1998.

Dummelow, J. R. *One Volume Bible Commentary.* New York: Macmillan, 1908.

Eyring, Henry B. Conference Report, April 2006, 13–17.

Faust, James E. Conference Report, October 2005, 19–22.

Groberg, John H. Conference Report, April 2001, 56–58.

Hinckley, Gordon B. Conference Report, April 1995, 91–95.

———. Conference Report, April 1998, 3–5.

———. Conference Report, October 1987, 55–59.

———. *The Teachings of Gordon B. Hinckley.* Salt Lake City: Deseret Book, 1997.

———. Worldwide Leadership Training Broadcast, 10 January 2004.

Holland, Jeffrey R. Conference Report, April 1983, 51–54.

Hunter, Howard W. Conference Report, October 1994, 66–70.

Hymns of The Church of Jesus Christ of Latter-day Saints. Salt Lake City: The Church of Jesus Christ of Latter-day Saints, 1985.

References

Journal of Discourses. 26 volumes. London: Latter-day Saints Book Depot, 1854-86.

Kelly, James. "We're Not Going to Make It," *Time,* 25 January 1982, 16-17.

Kimball, Spencer W. "Hold Fast to the Iron Rod," *Ensign,* November 1978, 4-6.

Lee, Harold B. "Be Loyal to the Royal Within You." Address, Brigham Young University, September 11, 1973. In *Speeches of the Year: BYU Devotional and Ten-Stake Fireside Addresses, 1973.* Provo, Utah: BYU Press, 1973, 85-103.

——. Conference Report, April 1973, 176-81.

——. "The Place of the Priesthood Quorum in the Church Security Program," *Improvement Era,* October 1937, 634-35.

——. *Stand Ye in Holy Places.* Salt Lake City: Deseret Book, 1974.

MacArthur, John. *The Freedom and Power of Forgiveness.* Wheaton, Ill.: Crossway Books, 1998.

McConkie, Bruce R. Conference Report, April 1985, 9-12.

——. Conference Report, October 1977, 49-53.

——. *The Mortal Messiah.* 4 vols. Salt Lake City: Deseret Book, 1981.

——. "Only an Elder," *Ensign,* June 1975, 66-69.

——. *A New Witness for the Articles of Faith.* Salt Lake City: Deseret Book, 1985.

McConkie, Joseph Fielding. *Understanding the Power God Gives Us.* Salt Lake City: Deseret Book, 2004.

McKay, David O. *Gospel Ideals.* Salt Lake City: Improvement Era, 1953.

Monson, Thomas S. Conference Report, April 2006, 56-61.

Muggeridge, Malcolm. *Jesus: The Man Who Lives.* New York: Harper & Row, 1975.

Oaks, Dallin H. Conference Report, April 1986, 65-70.

Packer, Boyd K. "Teaching: The Moral Standard," Address to Church Educational System personnel, Brigham Young University, 15 July 1958.

——. Conference Report, October 1987, 17-21.

——. *The Holy Temple.* Salt Lake City: Bookcraft, 1980.

——. "On the Shoulders of Giants," J. Reuben Clark Law Society devotional address, Brigham Young University, 28 February 2004.

Pratt, Parley P. *Autobiography of Parley P. Pratt.* Salt Lake City: Deseret Book, 1938.

Richards, Stephen L. Conference Report, October 1938, 114-19.

Rosenblatt, Roger. "The Man in the Water," *Time,* 25 January 1982, 86-87.

Smith, Joseph. *Lectures on Faith.* Salt Lake City: Deseret Book, 1985.

———. *Teachings of the Prophet Joseph Smith.* Compiled by Joseph Fielding Smith. Salt Lake City: Deseret Book, 1976.

Smith, Joseph F. *Gospel Doctrine.* Salt Lake City: Deseret Book, 1986.

———. *Teachings of the Presidents of the Church—Joseph F. Smith.* Salt Lake City: The Church of Jesus Christ of Latter-day Saints, 1998.

Smith, Joseph Fielding. Conference Report, April 1967, 119–23.

Talmage, James E. *Jesus the Christ.* Salt Lake City: Deseret Book, 1972.

Whitney, Orson F. Conference Report, April 1928, 56–61.

Wirthlin, Joseph B. Conference Report, October 2005, 14–18.

INDEX

meeting speaker, 120–21; by
being flippant, sacrilegious,
and irreverent, 120–24;
without using profanity,
121–22; Joseph Smith on
approaching perfection, 122;
Joseph Smith on
comprehending the character
of God, 122; Joseph Smith on
the importance of the things
of God, 122; reverence for
God's creations as reverence
for God, 122–23; acting in
God's name as a sacred trust,
124; Spencer W. Kimball on
making the Lord's name
important in your life, 124–25;
singing praises to God's name,
125; sacred responsibility of
priesthood holders to avoid,
125–26
Taylor, John, on achieving oneness,
64–65
Television sitcoms, distorted
portrayals of fathers in, 11
Thoughts, eternal, 34–35
Treasuring the right things, 30–31.
See also Lesser things, avoiding

Unity: power of, 54, 57; experience
of moving into new branch
and raising money to build
chapel, 54–57; experience
taking young son to visit Baker
Ward, 57–58; power of

priesthood quorums, 58–60;
with those of other faiths,
61–63; achieving unity in spite
of diversity, 64; John Taylor on,
64–65; experience with ward
members fasting on behalf of
ill high priest, 65–67

Valor, characteristics of, 2
Vulgarity. *See* Taking God's name in
vain

Whitney, Orson F., on uniting with
those of other faiths in God's
work, 61
Wilkinson, Harold, 9
Wirthlin, Joseph B., on the journey
to higher ground, 17–18
Women: Christ's treatment of, 72;
priesthood holders'
responsibility to create an
atmosphere of love, trust,
intimacy, and respect, 72–73;
exercising priesthood
authority within bounds set by
the Lord, 73–74
Woodruff, Wilford, raises wife from
the dead, 92–93
Wrongs of life: to be righted by the
power of the Atonement,
80–81; Boyd K. Packer on
surviving, 81–82

Young, Brigham, on being
righteous in the dark, 84

ABOUT THE AUTHOR

Robert L. Millet, professor of ancient scripture and former dean of Religious Education at Brigham Young University, has served with Church Public Affairs and the Materials Evaluation Committee of The Church of Jesus Christ of Latter-day Saints.

He is the author of numerous books, including *Grace Works, Are We There Yet?* and *When a Child Wanders.* He is also the coauthor with Lloyd D. Newell of a daily devotional series of books: *Jesus, the Very Thought of Thee; When Ye Shall Receive These Things; Draw Near Unto Me;* and *A Lamp Unto My Feet.*

Brother Millet and his wife, Shauna, are the parents of six children and reside in Orem, Utah.